Finding the Teacher Self

Finding the Teacher Self

Developing Your Teacher Identity through Critical Reflection

Eric Shyman

ROWMAN & LITTLEFIELD
Lanham • Boulder • New York • London

Published by Rowman & Littlefield
An imprint of The Rowman & Littlefield Publishing Group, Inc.
4501 Forbes Boulevard, Suite 200, Lanham, Maryland 20706
www.rowman.com

6 Tinworth Street, London SE11 5AL, United Kingdom

British Library Cataloguing in Publication Information Available

Library of Congress Cataloging-in-Publication Data

Names: Shyman, Eric, 1979– author.
Title: Finding the teacher self : developing your teacher identity through critical reflection / Eric Shyman.
Description: Lanham : Rowman & Littlefield, [2020] | Includes bibliographical references. | Summary: "This offers a foundation to begin and sustain a discussion with preservice and in-service teachers about the role of teacher identities in the classrooms, what their teacher identity is, and how they can continue to develop it"— Provided by publisher.
Identifiers: LCCN 2019059513 (print) | LCCN 2019059514 (ebook) | ISBN 9781475853193 (cloth) | ISBN 9781475853209 (paperback) | ISBN 9781475853216 (epub)
Subjects: LCSH: Reflective teaching—United States. | Critical pedagogy—United States. | Culturally relevant pedagogy—United States. | Identity (Psychology)—United States. | Teachers—Training of—United States. | Teachers—In-service training—United States.
Classification: LCC LB1025.3 .S5424 2020 (print) | LCC LB1025.3 (ebook) | DDC 371.14/4—dc23
LC record available at https://lccn.loc.gov/2019059513
LC ebook record available at https://lccn.loc.gov/2019059514

∞™ The paper used in this publication meets the minimum requirements of American National Standard for Information Sciences—Permanence of Paper for Printed Library Materials, ANSI/NISO Z39.48-1992.

For Lori, Nathan, and Lucas

Contents

Acknowledgments

There are many people to whom I owe much gratitude in the production of this book. First are Tom Koerner and Carlie Wall of Rowman & Littlefield Publishers, without whom publication would not be possible. Also to my wife, Lori, whose love and tolerance of me as a writer, thinker, dad, and husband means everything. To my older son, Nathan, whose intellect and curiosity impress me daily, and who continues to ask the most meaningful questions that inform my own thinking all the time. To my younger son, Lucas, whose love, affection, and gentle nature make me never forget that I am, above all things, a dad. I owe my very life to my mother, Wendy, and late father, Paul.

To all of the wonderful scholars, thinkers, and teachers whose work informs and gives meaning to my own study and teaching invaluably: I humbly thank you. And finally, to all my students: those whom I have had in class, those whom I currently have in class, and those whom I will have in class in the future. It is you all who continue to teach more than I can ever teach another, and you who keep me motivated and dedicated to the field I love so deeply and dearly, education.

Preface

"WE TEACH ANYWAY"[1]

There are many reasons why I wrote this book. Education is in constant fluctuation, such that, in a sense, there cannot be education without simultaneous education reform. I have even argued in past writing that American education is synonymous with education reform and has been since the beginning of the American public school system. On a larger scale, politicians and policy makers are ever discussing what is wrong with our schools, and occasionally, though far more seldom, what is right.

On a smaller scale, teachers are reflecting every day, sometimes every moment if they are skilled enough, to determine what worked, what didn't, why it didn't, and what they can do next time to make it work. This smaller-scale reform is what some of us call reflection, or more aptly reflective practice, and it is the centerpiece of teachers who can truly be deemed effective. This is not effectiveness based on some prescribed metric, or rubric, or evaluation criteria. Rather, this is effectiveness based on the teacher who can wade through the policy, the administrative distraction, the sound bites and the paperwork, and, as the great teacher Rita Pierson said, "teach anyway."

People talk much about teachers. Often it is negative, composed of comments suggesting that teachers are glorified babysitters, failed practitioners in the field in which they teach, unable to get another, real job in that field, union apologists, and underworked, overpaid talkers who get their summers off and three paid vacations per year. These are common but deeply misinformed invectives that teachers are regularly forced to endure on a nearly daily basis, and given little, if any, real opportunity to respond.

When asked what we do, and we answer that we are teachers, there is the familiar smirk that appears on those to whom we are talking. We know what they are thinking, and we know that they are wrong. "Taxpayers" accost us at school board meetings and in the community, believing that because they contribute money with which our salaries are paid, and have experienced schools themselves in one way or another, they know what it is we should be doing, and why what we are doing is always somehow wrong.

Still, through all of it, teachers are much more than this. While we endure the talk about us, seldom the chance to respond, we return to work daily and often with excitement, with the future of our culture and our country, quite literally at times, in our hands. We handle the emotional remnants of the TV news report one of our immigrant students heard and now fears that she will be sent back to her country, with or without the rest of her family. We handle the questions one of our Muslim students had because he heard in the grocery store that Arabs hate America, and that "we should all be very careful of them if we see them." We handle the confusion of the white children and black children who are unsure what their differences are but have somehow learned that they are there, and they should be important.

And we handle these issues all in one place that we are expected to keep safe, constructive, and productive regardless of what people say about us. And after all of this—then comes the content.

The deluge of regulations, standardizations, assessments, evaluations, documentations, curriculum materials, copy-making, grading, team meetings, IEP goal progress monitoring, duties, and preparations is seemingly interminable. Our long, late nights lead to early mornings with the best-case scenario being to just stay caught up enough, knowing that whatever it is we did can and probably will change, again, at the drop of a hat with little, if any, input from us. We are professionals who are done to and done for. Nevertheless, as Rita Pierson said, "we teach anyway."

There is a reason, and a strong one, why we teach anyway. It is because we love children, we believe in education, and we believe in a world that, though it cannot be perfect, can be better, and the betterment comes from education. We, as teachers, are described perfectly by Neil Postman and Charles Weingartner, who said,

> We are serious, dedicated, professional educators, which means that we are simple, romantic men and women who risk contributing to the problems of the world by maintaining a belief in the improvability of the human condition through education. We are not so simple and romantic as to believe that all of the problems we have enumerated are susceptible to solution—through education or anything else. But some can be solved, and perhaps more directly through education than other means.[2]

The potential irony that this quote comes from a book written in 1971 criticizing "outdated teaching methods" is not lost, but in fact captures the very heart of the argument of this book. That is, good teaching is not necessarily about "keeping up" or "staying current," nor is bad teaching simply about maintaining instructional practices that are simply irrelevant, no longer effective, or have never been effective. Rather, it is about teachers perpetually thinking about teaching, why they are teaching, what they are teaching, to whom they are teaching it, and who told them what to teach what they are teaching. In a word, it is about reflection.

Reflection is a concept that is easily dismissed, and has often been, as mere intellectualism or rationalization. An arbitrary and self-serving process that works only to reinforce what one already believes: that one is doing the best they can. In reality this dismissal is not valid. Reflection, when engaged in correctly and systematically, is a deeply uprooting and disruptive process, more comfortable to avoid than to embrace.

The fact is that the dialogue about teaching at the conversational and political levels gets lost in "contemporary" issues, losing sight of the fact that those issues identified are merely current outplays of deep-seated, systemic, cultural problems that will remain, unless they are named, addressed, and solved in a way that considers the validity and contribution of all possible narratives.

What, then, are narratives? Narratives serve a central function in the exploration undertaken in this book. They are the source from which our personal opinions, beliefs, sense of truth, and preconceptions develop. These are the stories told to us from the very beginning of our lives, before we could even understand them, and they frame each thing we do. They provide a context for our relationships, our identities, our sense of right and wrong, and our willingness to become involved in something or not. Indeed, we all have them, and we all function within them to one degree or another.

This is not the problem. The problem comes when we neglect to understand that these narratives are simply the ones we have; the ones, more aptly, that we were given. We can accept them and pass them on unquestioned and unevaluated. Present them as the truth and the way in which life should be lived and our experiences contextualized. Or we could hold them dear, but at the same time critique them, expand them, delete elements from them, and add elements to them. Conjoin them and intertwine them with others' stories and weave a long and wide tapestry with them.

This is what this book is essentially about: how do we take the elements of our lives that often go unnamed, unnoticed, and unexamined and make sense of them in the context of who we are as teachers? We often hold on so tightly to our identities in our personal lives: we are sons, daughters, fathers, mothers, liberals, conservatives, Democrats, Republicans, Jews, Muslims, and Christians. Yet in our professions, we do not take the time to develop our identities, or even see the need to do so. This book will create a pathway, indeed, just one pathway, that can help teachers examine who it is they are as teachers, and how who they are as teachers extends from who they are as people.

This book is not set forth as a manual or textbook. Rather, it is to serve as but one piece of an ever-expanding and expandable puzzle that is the professional teacher. It is, essentially, a workbook of sorts. A book that poses questions with the intention that they will lead to better questions, more complex and compounding questions that require more complex and compounding research. A book that will hopefully be reread and revisited many times, allowing the teacher to notice his or her own growth measured by the differences in which the questions are answered or understood or framed. A book that can be taken in many directions and be contributed to by many and varying perspectives. Indeed, I hope this is what it becomes for any who read it.

NOTES

1. Rita Pierson. (2013). *Every Kid Needs a Champion.* Retrieved on October 13, 2019, from https://www.ted.com/talks/rita_pierson_every_kid_needs_a_champion.
2. Neil Postman and Charles Weingartner. (1971). *Teaching as a Subversive Activity: A No-Holds-Barred Assault on Outdated Teaching Methods with Dramatic and Practical Proposals on How Education Can Be Made Relevant to Today's World.* New York: Bantam Dell.

Introduction

The social and cultural setting in which this book was written is as important to consider as the arguments in the book itself. The United States is experiencing social and political stress and division that have not yet been experienced by its younger generations. Indeed, while many from the Vietnam era insist that it has been worse—that their youth was fraught with more upheaval, social unrest, violence, and outrage—the younger generations insist they are dealing with issues no other generation understands. And this is likely true.

The availability of mobile information technologies, social media, accessibility of cameras, mass data collection, and a myriad other unprecedented social, political, and technological issues are presenting challenges few, if any, quite know how to deal with. At the same time there is significant stratification of wealth, with the rich, who are now very rich, seeming only to get richer and everyone else struggling. There is talk of the middle class and whether it is vanishing, while some wonder whether it ever really existed. There are waxing and waning "Occupy" movements, struggles between capitalist and socialist political and economic ideologies, arguments over nationalism and patriotism, and a general decline in civil discourse that reaches the highest of political offices.

All the while, teachers and students are going to school and being expected to sort through all these issues, their resulting emotions and stresses, and still find room, and value, for academic content. But the content leads to even more questions. Who determined the content? And why did they decide this content was important? Who gave these decision makers the right or the privilege to make such decisions? And who was part of that decision-making process? Why does it seem that not only do the same problems still exist, but now there are new ones to add? There are children committing suicide.

There are children being bullied in school and online. There are children killing other children, and adults killing other adults. And there are also adults killing children and children killing adults. There is so much violence, yet all educational policy seems to talk about is college and career readiness, the so-called achievement gap, and our failing students, failing teachers, and failing schools. They prescribe curricula, standards, and certification requirements for teachers. Yet still there is no positive change.

Finding the Teacher Self: Developing Your Teacher Identity through Critical Reflection takes the opportunity to ask those questions that the policy makers and school administrators do not seem to be asking, or even interested in asking. It considers teaching not as an academic exercise intended to share academic knowledge, nor as a professional exercise intended to meet predetermined and prescribed goals superimposed upon teachers. Rather, it considers teaching as a sociopolitical and sociocultural act, responsible for creating the very society within school walls, as well as outside of them. In the context of teaching society, culture, and politics must be deeply explored and exposed in their realness and dirtiness, their inequality, injustice, and unflattering history; and it is done not out of anger, or bitterness, or resentment, but in service of progress. To address and solve real social, cultural, and political problems is to expose them and name them, honestly evaluate them, and survey their consequences in the actually lived lives of people whom they affect. And this is all facilitated through the process of reflection.

In truth this work is at once broad and narrow. It is broad in the sense that it takes on the teaching profession as a whole, from preservice teachers to experienced in-service teachers, making room for the wealth of experiences that each group has. While the older teachers have classroom time and reform survival stories to share, the younger teachers have fresh experiences navigating a new and complicating world, and ones that match their students' world far better than do the older generations'. It is broad in the sense that it takes on multiple sociocultural issues such as race, ethnicity, gender, sexuality, political ideology, and even religion in some contexts, and it attempts to break these identities apart in service of piecing them together again differently and more purposefully.

It is narrow in the sense that it attempts to pay attention to the details and nuances of the more complex issues requiring the readers to take their thoughts, beliefs, and conceptions and dissect them into even the smallest parts. It tugs at the sensitive elements of one's personal identity and cultural affiliations, political and moral leanings, sense of value and virtue, and, most importantly, one's biases and prejudices, which we all have though would rather avoid. This book can be personalized, allowing for very deep introspection and exploration of one's own mind. In this vein, it employs the word *finding* in its title to honor the idea that people are who they are, and that any critical change that may come about is often harkened by something that is "found" rather than something that is forced or deliberately created. People change, therefore, by gradually adjusting their core beliefs with their current reality and assimilating these adjustments in ways that are expansive and deepening, allowing themselves to see who they were, but still become who they are. This change may represent a shift in ideology, belief, or attitude such as a skinhead becoming nonracist or an executioner becoming opposed to the death penalty. But it is a deep change that affects one's very perspective.

These changes can be jarring, if not outright scary. We grasp our identities tightly and with vigor, and almost instinctively defend against any threat to them. Perhaps sometimes this is necessary—what keeps us who we are. But when these defenses become weakening or sheltering, disallowing us to understand or accept other perspectives or modes of thinking, causing us to feel resentment, or aversion, or avoidance, or anger, or even hate of another, this is when our identity betrays us. As teachers we do this often, and it makes us less effective teachers.

Reflection, then, as a systematic process, will prevent us from falling victim to our prejudices. By keeping them in our sights at all times—watching them, assessing them, monitoring how they work—we can begin to understand the roles they play, and whether these roles are helpful or harmful. We can see that who we are as people reflects who we are as teachers, and perhaps vice versa, and that some of those reflections may be wonderful, and others may be quite detrimental.

Lastly, this book represents an attempt to work against the "top-down" nature of American education reform and teacher qualification processes, which has always been largely misguided, profit-based, and punitive. Processes such as completion of the edTPA and corporate-driven competency tests exemplify this concept. In its place, I attempt to argue for thoughtful, systematic, and genuinely transformative self-improvement processes that authentically deepen both teacher and student educational experiences. Engaging in this process will result in a profound appreciation for and acquisition of knowledge that can be used to make truly meaningful improvements to an ever-complicating social, political, and cultural landscape, and shape the lives of people who will become true citizens.

In a sense this shift in focus represents a similar shift in my own intellectual and professional disposition. For many years I took what would be considered an adversarial approach to education reform, attempting to expose untruths and exploitations of current systems. While there is room for such writing and discussion, I have come to find that this approach often leads only to more conversation rather than affecting actual teaching practices. Wanting to potentially affect classrooms rather than just conversations, this book is an attempt to use the knowledge I gained from expository writing to directly inform the act of teacher self-improvement that highlights positive transformation.

Part I is designed to help teachers reflect on some of the social and cultural processes that have shaped them over their lives and careers. The chapters are written with small chunks of information followed by activities and discussion questions that can be facilitated on one's own or in larger groups, as a discussion or as an exercise. The questions are designed to prompt one to think deeper and wider and to question, gradually, who one is, or who one *thinks* one is, at one's very core. Elements such as personal identity, emotion, cultural affiliation, prejudice, and bias will come to the forefront and demand attention and exploration. It is through these processes that, if taken seriously, teachers can deepen their process of reflection.

Part II is designed to deepen the discussion of how the reflective teacher can apply what is learned from the reflection to actual classroom practice. Focusing on elements such as culturally responsive pedagogy, peace education, scholarship activism, action research, and service learning, teachers can learn not only how to deepen their own practice with reflection, but also how to foster a community of reflection for their own students.

Finally, it is important to name and discuss two elements inherent in this work. First is the naming of author bias. Indeed, as a human being that is largely a product of his society, my own biases are as much at work in my writing as they would be in anyone else's. In an attempt to make this book as objective as possible, I did my best to bracket my opinions and perspectives where possible. Whether this was successful is up to the reader more than it is up to me. However, the very content of the book will undoubtedly reveal much about my own thoughts and perspectives, if not ideological tendencies and beliefs. By sharing methodologies such as culturally responsive pedagogy, peace education, and service learning I am doubtless revealing my support of them, and this support may beckon other perceived biases by the reader as well, whether they are true or not.

Second is the role of language, and in particular its precariousness. While much care was taken to define, conceptualize, and contextualize the terms used, the meaning of much of the language used in the book can likely be subjective, or at least leave room for debate in both denotation and connotation. Therefore, the language itself must carefully considered.

As a result, I encourage those who engage with this book to make these two elements a direct part of their discussion. For example, how does my potential bias as an author "color" the content and the questions in the book? Perhaps groups may want to discuss these elements first in order to "neutralize" any possible bias-based residue left and build from there. Additionally, making the meaning of the words in question a part of the discussion itself can be helpful. For example, when I use the word "hegemony" to describe the dominant culture, is there agreement with how I am using this word or to whom I am referring by this word to begin with?

In either sense, the main purpose of this book is discussion, and the deeper and wider the discussion the better. This book can and should be supplemented with additional readings: readings that affirm the information and readings that challenge or oppose it. That is, the more that can be added to the discussion while maintaining its manageability can only help, and it is my hope and intention that this is how this book will be used.

Selected Works to Use Along with This Book

Janet Alsup. (2004). "Am I a Teacher? Exploring the Development of Professional Identity." *Language Arts Journal of Michigan, 20*(1), 35–39.

Kenneth Zeichner & Daniel P. Liston. (2013). *Reflective Teaching: An Introduction.* New York: Routledge.

Catherine Beauchamp & Lynn Thomas. (2009). "Understanding Teacher Identity: An Overview of Issues in the Literature and Implications for Teacher Education." *Cambridge Journal of Education, 39*(2), 175–189.

Robin DiAngelo. (2011). "White Fragility." *International Journal of Critical Pedagogy, 3*(3), 54–70.

Gerardo R. Lopez. (2003). "The (Racially Neutral) Politics of Education: A Critical Race Theory Perspective." *Educational Administration Quarterly, 39*(1), 68–94.

Ana Maria Villegas & Tamara Lucas. (2007). "The Culturally Responsive Teacher." *Educational Leadership, 64*(6), 28–33.

Zeus Leonardo. (2004). "The Color of Supremacy: Beyond the Discourse of 'White Privilege.'" *Educational Philosophy and Theory, 36*(2), 137–152.

Gloria Ladson-Billings. (2005). *Beyond the Big House: African American Educators on Teacher Education.* New York: Teachers College Press.

Lisa Delpit. (2019). *Teaching When the World Is on Fire.* New York: The New Press.

Mack T. Hines, III. (2017). *White Teachers, Black Students: In the Spirit of Yes to African American Student Achievement.* Lanham, MD: Rowman & Littlefield Publishers.

Marilyn Cochran-Smith. (2018). *Reclaiming Accountability in Teacher Education.* New York: Teachers College Press.

Part I

BECOMING A REFLECTIVE TEACHER

Chapter One

The Teaching Mirror

What Is Reflective Teaching and Why Is It Important?

"Reflective teachers are continually asking themselves why they are doing what they are doing."[1]

—Kenneth Zeichner and Daniel Liston

WHAT IS REFLECTIVE TEACHING?

Many concepts offer intrigue just based on what they are called but offer little in terms of actual innovation when scratched beneath the surface. Reflective teaching is not such a concept. While the term "reflective teaching" is likely to mean different things to different people, and such differences may be quite valid and well-founded, there are certain essential elements for reflective teaching to be practicable and useful. Reflective teaching, then, must be seen as a continuum that can be engaged in a multitude of ways. As J. John Loughran describes it:

> Reflective practice has an allure that is seductive in nature because it rings true for most people as something useful and informing. However, for reflection to genuinely be a lens into the world of practice, it is important the nature of reflection be identified in such a way as to offer ways of questioning taken-for-granted assumptions and encouraging one to see his or her practice through others' eyes.[2]

What is central to the idea of reflection is the recognition and naming of problems, either within oneself or externally. The reflective teacher will then continuously and systematically address these problems, and one's relation and contribution to them, in service of the amelioration of that problem by adjusting one's own behavior and practice.

Reflective teachers recognize that the process of educating others represents a balance between one's technical knowledge (such as the academic curriculum and its corresponding standards), skill (knowledge and training in particular pedagogical systems and methods), and art (the ability to use one's classroom as a place of creation, extension, and deepening of the life experience such that it can continue even in its absence). This process, when implemented carefully and with thought, allows teachers to continuously redefine their roles, their knowledge, their expectations, and their presumptions within a dynamic environment, allowing always for the best possible means of addressing the behavioral, social, cultural, and academic needs of their students.

Historically, most scholars credit the advent of reflection in the professions, including teaching, to a groundbreaking work by Donald Schon called *The Reflective Practitioner: How Professionals Think in Action*.[3] However, Schon's ideas have been deepened and widened by a number of scholars in the field of education including, but not limited to, Kenneth Zeichner, Dan Liston, J. John Loughran, Geneva Gay, Gloria Ladson Billings, and Marilyn Cochran Smith, among a number of others.

This continued exploration of what it means to be a reflective teacher has not only added legitimacy to the project itself, but has allowed many facets of the teaching profession to be transformed in ways that have contributed to progress in vital social, cultural, political, and socioeconomic areas.

HOW DO I "DO" REFLECTIVE TEACHING?

On the coattails of the question *what is reflective teaching*, however, comes an additional, if not deeper question of, *how does one engage in reflective teaching*? This question, indeed, comprises the bulk of this book. But it is important, at the outset, to begin to get a sense of what may be involved in embarking on such a journey that can be, at times, so elusive to capture and define.

Perhaps a good point at which to start is by exploring what J. John Loughran calls "making the tacit explicit."[4] By this Loughran means that when teaching becomes automatic, it also runs the risk of becoming thoughtless, and we, as teachers, cease to think about what we are doing, and risk just doing it out of habit. Many reflective practitioners and scholars may refer to this juncture as somewhat of a "danger zone" in which one may not only stop being effective as a teacher but become a contributor to the many deep and complex problems that arise in the teaching process.

Teachers can begin to "make the tacit explicit" by engaging in, at first, a relatively simple exercise in which they hold themselves (or their various identities) up to a proverbial mirror and simply state what they see. For example:

1. I am a teacher.
2. I am a woman/man.
3. I am white/black/brown skinned.
4. I am a constructivist/behaviorist.
5. I am a conservative/liberal.
6. I teach mostly white/black/brown children.
7. I believe homework is/is not valuable.

By engaging in a basic reflective activity such as this, reflective teachers can learn two main things about themselves. First, what is thought of first is likely the most significant "characteristic" or "label" at the given moment. This realization alone provides much fodder for deeper reflection (why did I label myself "that" first; what does "that" mean to me; when and how did I become "that"?). Second, it allows one to begin to recognize what the structure of one's cultural system, and therefore value system, is.

PRACTICE: NAMING YOUR TEACHER THOUGHT PROCESSES

1. What does it mean to me to *be* a teacher? What does a teacher *do*?
2. What role does my gender play in my teaching? What about my students' gender?
3. What does my skin color indicate about my cultural beliefs and experiences? What about my students' skin color and their beliefs and experiences?
4. What does it mean to identify with a teaching "paradigm"? In what ways does this identification limit my teaching? In what ways does it expand it?
5. How do my political or ideological beliefs as a liberal/conservative affect the way in which I interact with my students? What if I am teaching about a topic that I have an ideological conflict about? What role does my ideology play?
6. What role does my students' skin color play as compared to my own? Does it matter if it is different or the same? In what ways might it matter that I don't yet realize?
7. Do I consider what "home" is like for students when I give them "homework"? Are there any assumptions that accompany my assignment of homework? What consequences do I inflict for students who do not complete homework? Are these consequences just, and how might I know?

The words one uses to label one's identity are always indicative of the culture or cultures with which one identifies, and those cultures, in turn, contribute significantly to (if not entirely construct) one's value system, thus allowing one to assess what is right or wrong, good or bad, worthy or unworthy. These judgments invariably affect our classroom beliefs and practices and often reveal elements of our teaching styles in which we simply engaged without ever thinking about it.

To take this idea a bit deeper, one can now relook at one's "list of identities" and begin to pose questions to oneself about them.

When reflection is engaged in constructively, the teacher is likely to find that the questions lead not to answers, or at least definitive ones, but only to more questions, and more avenues by which one can continue to reflect. Teachers, then, who end at what they think are the answers and view these activities as discrete practices have, in effect, stopped reflecting, and are likely to have missed the point of reflective practice to begin with.

WHY IS REFLECTIVE TEACHING IMPORTANT?

Perhaps one of the most common questions that busy, application-minded professionals like teachers ask is, essentially, "what's the point?" This is a fair question considering the multiple and ever-increasing demands on teachers in the 21st century and the limited decision latitude they are granted involving their roles to begin with. The best answer can be gathered by taking a slightly different and deeper look at the school environment, and the absolutely central role that teachers play in it.

Essentially, just as in the absence of doctors a hospital would be just another building, without teachers, there would be no school in any real sense. It is the teachers that form the very foundation of the school, facilitating *where* school happens, and *what* happens there. Indeed, a number of roles contribute to the functioning of a school or a school's administrative organization, but none is more foundational than the teacher.

Teachers work with, and within, curriculums. Every decision a teacher makes, every word a teacher says, every activity a teacher provides, and every assignment and activity a teacher implements formulates what becomes the curriculums of the school. The key to understanding curriculums, however, is that there can be two main types: the blatant and the tacit. The blatant curriculum is composed of what teachers *know* they are implementing (such as academic instruction, behavior management, functional, or life-based skills).

The tacit curriculum, sometimes called the "hidden curriculum,"[5] comprises the social, cultural, and even political messages that teachers unintentionally, or unwittingly, give. It is with this information that only reflective teachers are able to work, because without reflection, this curriculum, its contents, and its consequences remain hidden and, therefore, both undetected and perpetuated.

Central and building-level administrators, as well as other school personnel such as security, also contribute in deep ways to the school's tacit curriculum. The presence of metal detectors at school entrances, the conducting of locker searches in random or targeted fashion, the involvement of police in disciplinary issues, and the hierarchy of handling disciplinary matters (such as whether such processes are part of the principal's or assistant principal's purview or whether there is a designated "dean" or other such position for disciplinary issues in particular) are all cultural artifacts that perpetuate clear messages with either their presence or absence.

Marshall McLuhan, a social commentator, once suggested "the medium is the message."[6] What he meant by this is that *how* a message is sent can be more important than *what* is said. That is, the presence of metal detectors in elementary or middle schools sends a clear message to the students that they are perceived as criminals sight unseen, whereas the absence of such items implicates trust in their lack of "necessity." These media, and the messages they send, find their most authoritative voice through school and classroom policy, all of which, essentially, is conducted through the classroom with the teacher as its "face."

There is an additional reason as to why reflective practice is so critical, but it bears the burden of needing somewhat of an introduction, especially given the general climate of "Westernized" societies. Few topics are susceptible to more controversy, dissension, avoidance, and even verbal or political "warfare" as that of race and ethnicity. To legitimize why the discussion of race and ethnicity is essential, let's consider some findings. In a 2014 report, the Center for American Progress claimed that while 40 percent of the school-age population is composed of students of color, only 17 percent of the teacher force is composed of teachers of color.

This means that the vast majority of students, white or of color, are taught by white teachers. Additionally, these trends appear to be growing, deepening the diversity gap between the teacher force and the student body at a national level, with more diverse states such as California, Nevada, and New York showing even larger gaps.[7] Similar findings are reported in Europe[8,9] and have been replicated by multiple outlets. Similarly, between 87 and 93 percent of school principals are also white, and 93 percent of school superintendents are white.[10,11]

It is safe to claim, then, that white teachers and administrators at both the building and central levels comprise the dominant group in schools and, therefore, bring with them the cultural representations and expectations of the white community, along with the prejudgments, biases, and cultural ignorance of other cultures' communities. Perhaps the reader recoiled at this sentence. After all, there appeared to be an accusation of prejudgment, bias, and worst of all, ignorance.

This language is very intentional, however, and comfort with it, as well as acceptance of it, is incumbent on being a truly reflective teacher. While this language will be developed and explored more deeply, suffice it to suggest, at this point, that these words are not insulting, nor indicative of "badness" in any way. Rather, they are a consequence of the deep and incontrovertible institution of neighborhood-based segregation in the United States.

Because this lack of cultural integration is combined with the notion of authority placed upon teachers and administrators in a school, it is virtually unavoidable that the cultural expectations of the dominant group will become the "rules" of the environment. That is, social rules are typically seen as "fixed" by those who hold them. Therefore, violations of the social rules should be corrected by means of behavior management and classroom codes of conduct (for example, raising one's hand is required to engage, whereas calling out is corrected and perhaps disciplined). Once this system of rewards and punishments becomes ingrained in the culture, the resulting behavior either follows suit, and is rewarded, or does not, and is punished.

This concept is equally important, however, for culturally dominant teachers working in culturally dominant communities. Just as the rules of the dominant culture are superimposed on the educational context for students within a different culture who may hold different cultural values and social practices, the common social rules between like cultures will also be reinforced. That is, when white teachers work with predominantly white children and reinforce the same cultural rules as dictated by the greater white community, the "rightness" of these rules is perpetuated, if not concretized.

This disables these students from understanding, in any real way, that the rules they see as "fixed" are actually just perceptions and can be refuted. When confronted with another individual or group of individuals, especially if different in terms of skin color, religion, ethnicity, or nationality, the white students will have no referent for behavior other than their own, immediately relegating the "others" as wrong, or misbehaved, and themselves as "right," or socially acceptable. Consider the following thought experiment.

This brief thought experiment is intended to accentuate the deep differences between cultural traditions that can result in stark inconsistencies in behavior, especially as it applies to situations considered "reverent," in which the showing of respect, engagement, and "social codes" is significant, such as church and school. If these differences are not understood in a manner

It is fair to say that many individuals view the roots of their behavior from a religious standpoint. That is, how one is supposed to act at one's house of worship can be generalized to how one should act in any other environment. Indeed, if it is okay in a "house of God," it is likely okay elsewhere. However, while the roots of one's belief system may share commonality, the corresponding behavior within such an environment may be starkly different. Picture a house of worship that predominantly white worshippers attend. This may be a Catholic or Protestant church or a Jewish temple. What is the general code of conduct here? Is one to shout during the service? Is one to dance, or clap, or interrupt the officiant with exclamations? Likely not, and so it is not done, and therefore seen as the model of decorum for other such "serious" interactions. Now picture a house of worship that predominantly black worshippers attend. Are the rules the same? What about the behavior? What might this tell you about how these worshippers perceive the behavioral or social norms of other environments based on their own church? How does this challenge your sense of your own "rightness" in the norms of social behavior?

separate from *right* or *wrong*, *appropriate* or *inappropriate*, it is always the dominant perspective that reigns, creating all other belief and behavior systems to be regarded as deficient and, therefore, needing correction.[12]

Think of how this presumption, as unaware as you are (or were) of it, underscores almost everything you do in your classroom and colors every interaction with your students regardless of your cultural commonality with them; how the very definition of "engagement" or "answering" or "reverence" could be opposed, and the danger of the resulting cultural consequence.[13] Once you are able to acknowledge this, and these types of situations, as a problem, but also as a means for deeper understanding and practice, you have begun to understand the virtue, and the power, of reflective teaching.

So now that the basic understanding of reflective teaching has been achieved and you have already become familiar with the value that it can have, take yourself just a bit deeper by considering some admonitions:

1. Reflective teachers must recognize certain aspects of their teaching as *problems*.
2. Reflective teachers must accept that one has preconceptions, presumptions, prejudices, biases, and ignorance upon which one acts, tacitly or explicitly, in virtually every educational interaction.
3. Reflective teachers recognize that they have an unnamed set of social and cultural rules by which they abide and hold as the standard for others' behavior.

PRACTICE: TAKING IT DEEPER

Ms. T had done some reflection in her graduate studies, but since she's been practicing as a teacher she doesn't see the point anymore. She's too busy, she knows what she's doing, and it seems like the kind of thing you do in school, not in real teaching practice. Her principal disagrees, though, and encourages her to continue try to reflect, at least informally, regularly.

1. The author gave some suggestions for how reflective teaching should be defined. Critique those definitions in terms of your own practice and philosophies. What was missed in those definitions? What should be removed? What might you change about them? Explain all of these answers in your own terms.
2. An example of a series of questions that reflective teachers may ask themselves was suggested in the "What Is Reflective Teaching?" section. Of those questions, which three do you think are the most important to ask? Why did you choose those? What would be your answer to each of them?
3. Subsequent chapters will deal more deeply with the notion of cultural expectations and its potential effect on teaching. To begin to gain comfort with this idea, try to determine what culture(s) you feel you belong to. What would you name that culture? What are two words you may use to describe that culture? In what ways do those words apply to you?

4. Reflective teachers must remember that reflection is something that is easy to do poorly, and is not the same as "venting," "rationalizing," "backing up with data," or "speaking out of experience."

In fact, these examples are likely to be antagonistic to the true process of reflective teaching.

NOTES

1. Kenneth M. Zeichner & D. P. Liston. (2013). *Reflective Teaching: An Introduction*. New York: Routledge, p. 11.
2. J. John Loughran (2002). "Effective Reflective Practice: In Search of Meaning in Learning about Teaching." *Journal of Teacher Education*, *53*(1), 33–43.
3. Donald Schon. (1983). *The Reflective Practitioner: How Professionals Think in Action*. New York: Basic Books.
4. Loughran, 2002, p. 35.

5. P. P. Bilbao, P. I. Lucido, T.C. Iringan, & R. B. Javier. (2008). *Curriculum Development*. Philippines: Lorimar Publishing Inc.

6. Marshall McLuhan. (1964). *Understanding Media: The Extensions of Man*. New York: Mentor.

7. Ulrich Boser. (2014). Center for American Progress. Retrieved from https://eric.ed.gov/?id=ED564608.

8. A. Flintoff, A. Chappell, C. Gower et al. (2008). *Black and Minority Ethnic Trainees' Experiences of Physical Education Initial Teacher Training. Report to the Training and Development Agency*. Carnegie Research Institute, Leeds Metropolitan University. Retrieved from https://bura.brunel.ac.uk/bitstream/2438/4693/1/Fulltext.pdf.

9. Sigrid Luchtenberg. (2004). "Ethnic Diversity and Citizenship Education in Germany." In J. A. Banks, *Diversity and Citizenship Education: Global Perspectives*, 245–271. San Fransisco: Jossey-Bass.

10. United States Department of Education. (2016). *Trends in Public and Private School Principal Demographics and Qualifications: 1987–88 and 2011–12*. Retrieved October 11, 2019, from https://nces.ed.gov/pubs2016/2016189.pdf.

11. The School Superintendents Association. (2018). *2017–18 AASA Superintendent Salary and Benefits Study*. Retrieved October 11, 2019, from https://aasa.org/uploadedFiles/Policy_and_Advocacy/Final%20Report%202017-18%20Non-Member.pdf.

12. Carla R. Monroe. (2006). "African American Boys and the Discipline Gap: Balancing Educators' Uneven Hand." *Educational Horizons*, *84*(2), 102–111.

13. Lisa Delpit. (2006). "Lessons from Teachers." *Journal of Teacher Education*, *57*(3), 220–231.

Chapter Two

Who Am I Really?

Framing and Forming Your Teacher Identity

"The longest journey that you will make in your life is from your head to your heart."[1]

—Sioux Indian proverb

WHAT DO I REFLECT ON?

While reflection as a process is clearly important, it often begs for an object or concept on which it could be centered. That is, one is likely to ask "on what should I reflect?" Indeed, there are innumerable worthy aspects of teaching upon which one could reflect deeply. In this work, however, it will be argued that reflecting on the formation of a teacher identity is, perhaps, one of the most fruitful ways in which one can engage in the reflection process, and there are a few reasons why.

First, you develop a teacher identity whether you do so intentionally and reflectively or not. Second, who you are as a teacher, or what may be called your identity, is directly related to how you will engage in the teaching (and likely learning) process. Third, if there are elements of your teacher identity that consistently work against you, reflection upon their existence and solutions is the only possible way that such elements can change. Essentially, every teacher creates a "teacher self." As reflective teaching scholar Janet Alsup puts it:

> I couldn't figure out how to place myself in the classroom—who was I as a teacher? How much of my old self could I bring to my class? How much of

a new persona, almost a new person, did I have to create in order to interact with my students? I felt disoriented and a little off-balance. I didn't know how to be a teacher, even though I knew the fundamentals of a teacher's work. In short, I struggled with assuming a teacher identity.[2]

In this exemplary piece of self-reflection, Alsup engages in a mode of self-questioning that cuts right to the heart of her struggle as a new teacher: who she is when she walks into the classroom, and whom she will develop into as she remains and functions there. She also explores who of her existing self, that is her "non-teacher self" should play into who her new "teacher self" should be. This is all while keeping her focus on what appears to be her main goal as a teacher: interacting with her students.

In this short reflection we can observe a thoughtful teacher courageously opening herself up to the potential torment of self-reflection in order to interrogate the very roots of her identity and do so in order to become a better teacher. To better engage in this process of dissecting and splicing elements of one's "multiple selves" to create a new yet always developing "whole" Alsup proffers the concept of *borderlands*. This idea suggests that there are many elements of the self that stride both one's professional and personal identities, and that can each be used productively to inform the other.

For me, two important borderlands identities are those of a father and teacher. As a father, I am able to impart experiences onto younger teacher candidates who are not parents what it feels like to be playing the role of a father interacting with a teacher in an educational environment (the environment in which I am more established and comfortable as a teacher). The experience I undergo as a father is the result of an identity that was only somewhat recently assumed, at least respective to when my identity as a teacher was assumed.

More importantly, however, are the ways in which my role as a father informs my role as a teacher, and vice versa. I cannot separate these elements of my identity, try as I might, so the best experience to make of it is to allow their intermingling and informing of one another to deepen both in a constructive way.

As a teacher learning how to engage in self-reflection, the role of borderlands proves to be a fruitful source from which one can start, because it allows the teacher to simply observe and name the different roles he or she plays in his or her personal and professional lives, and gradually will allow for a deeper exploration, reflection, and analysis of how these roles interact, if at all.

Naming one's borderland identity is the start of a very constructive line of self-reflection, and one that can be taken much deeper. Before that, how-

PRACTICE: NAME YOUR BORDERLANDS

In the space below, try to simply name four elements of your *borderland* identity, or those aspects of your personal and professional lives that inform one another.

1. ______________________________
2. ______________________________
3. ______________________________
4. ______________________________

ever, it is important to take another look at your borderland identities once or twice more before you move on. Are there any identities you forgot to include and would like to add? Are there any that you would like to eliminate or replace?

Remember, the self-reflection process is continuous and ever-changing, so what you determine to be among your borderland identities today may be different than tomorrow, in a month, a year, or even by the end of this sentence. Consistently returning to these identities will allow you to continue the development of your teacher identity.

Now that you have grown more comfortable with your current choices of your borderland identities, it is important to deepen their development, and determine how, or in what way, each identity informs the other. In order to be truly constructive borderland identities, it is necessary that the roles interact with and inform one another in an original way. That is, the one identity informs the other in ways that only *it* could. For example, my experience as a father has informed my experience as a teacher by showing me the level and depth of emotion that fathers feel for their children, and how my words and tone as a teacher are central to the way in which a parent will receive, process, and understand the information I present.

This type of information cannot be provided by any identity other than that of a father. Conversely, my role as a teacher allows me to receive, process, and understand the information given to me about my children from their teachers' perspective (that is, as a teacher, not a parent). In this way, my experience as a teacher giving this information to other parents cannot be provided by any other role.

PRACTICE: ANALYZE YOUR BORDERLANDS

In the space below, revisit the four elements of your *borderland* identity. Try to identify one piece of information that can be provided *only* by nature of its identity.

1. ______________________________
2. ______________________________
3. ______________________________
4. ______________________________

CAPTURING TEACHER IDENTITY

While people often prefer to define concepts before engaging with them, such a practice is often counterproductive in reflection. That is, it is often the definition itself that prevents us from personally connecting to a concept and applying it to ourselves in service of trying to remain true to the conceptualization. If we try to determine *what* teacher identity *is* too quickly, we may risk simply trying to fulfill that definition. Rather, if we insert ourselves into the concept first and gain our own understanding, we are more ready to adapt the concept of teacher identity to where we already are as teachers.

The role that teacher identity plays in a teacher's life has been explored through many lenses. Teacher identity may inform the narratives that teachers create for themselves, the discourse in which the teachers participate and produce, the metaphors they use to guide their own understanding of teaching, and the influence that external factors have on their teaching, among a number of others.[3] According to Sachs:

> Teacher professional identity then stands at the core of the teaching profession. It provides a framework for teachers to construct their own ideas of "how to be" and "how to act" and "how to understand" their work and their place in society. Importantly, teacher identity is not something that is fixed nor is it imposed; rather it is negotiated through experience and the sense that is made of that experience.[4]

Teacher identity, then, can be said to be composed of two main elements: beliefs and emotions, and how one makes sense of and applies one's beliefs and emotions to one's teaching comprises one's "teacher self."

Beliefs are elusive to capture conceptually and have, indeed, been addressed by multiple scholars in multiple fields, adding to their definitional elusiveness. That is, paradigmatic leanings and disciplinary underpinnings often influence how a term is itself defined, ironically adding to its elusiveness in the attempt to define it.[5] The attempt to conceptualize belief in the context of teaching has most certainly been addressed by a number of education scholars.

Virginia Richardson, a scholar who writes widely on teaching, cites beliefs as the most important component of teacher action. According to Richardson, beliefs can be defined as "psychologically held understandings, premises, or propositions about the world that are felt to be true."[6] Through these beliefs teachers will come to conclusions about their environment and add to what will become their personal narratives about teaching informed by these beliefs.

Frank Pajares adds to the conceptualization of beliefs by citing the importance of the inclusion of the word "about"—that is, *belief about intelligence, belief about gender differences*, etc. Therefore, the "foundational" nature of a belief in general is disregarded; rather, it is the subject of the belief that plays a more important role than the nature of belief itself. As Pajares summarizes the variety of conceptualizations of belief:

> The result is a view of belief that speaks to the individual's judgment of truth or falsity of a proposition, a judgment that can only be inferred from a collective understanding of what human beings say, intend, and do. The challenge is to assess each component so as to have confidence that the belief inferred is a reasonably accurate representation of that judgment.[7]

In this Pajares regards the role of evaluation as essential to forming a belief; that is, a belief begins as a judgment that is deemed "reasonably accurate" based on one's assessment of its veracity.

Emotions, which can be equally elusive to conceptualize, also play a key role in teacher identity. Two components of emotion, emotional geographies and emotional labor, will be focused on as foundational in conceptualizing teacher identity. *Emotional geographies*, as put forth by Andy Hargreaves, can be defined as "the spatial and experiential patterns of closeness and/or distance in human interactions and relationships that help create, configure, and color the feelings and emotions we experience about ourselves, our world and each other."[8] By this account emotions are relational and variable, and through their development will cause the person experiencing emotions to change along with them.

Michalinos Zembylas puts forth an additional element of emotion as it pertains to teacher identity:

PRACTICE: HARNESSING YOUR EMOTIONS

Beliefs and emotions play a key role in the development of your teacher identity. Complete the following sentences quickly, following your initial thoughts.

1. I experience my most steadfast beliefs in the area of _______________.
2. When someone challenges my beliefs I _______________.
3. The most difficult emotion for me is _______________.
4. When I feel this emotion I _______________.
5. When I experience this emotion at work I _______________.
6. This usually creates _______________.

> Teacher identity and emotion discourse are formed within specific school political arrangements, in relation to certain expectations and requirements, one that presumes a teacher should conform to particular emotional rules.[9]

In this definition Zembylas admonishes us that, though we as teachers may feel emotion, our freedom to express or act on such emotions has limitations that are dictated by both the school and greater social culture. Therefore, our emotional geographies are not used only to develop and understand our emotions and how they pertain to the multiple aspects of the world around us, but also to understand the relationships within a professional and political context, and use this information also to determine if, how, and when our emotions should be shared.

APPLYING THEORY TO THE DEVELOPMENT OF TEACHER IDENTITY

Perhaps the most contentious relationship among teachers is that with theory, and the role that theory plays in practice. While many teachers view their jobs as entirely practical, made up of a series of clinically based "action" decisions, deeper reflection often reveals that teachers do, indeed, carry with them a defined set of expectations, philosophies, and even theories that guide their actions and decision-making, however tacitly. Since theory does affect teacher action, and reflection is a form of teacher action, what theories apply to reflection?

Two valuable theories that apply directly to reflection in teachers are the *possible selves theory* and the *Foucauldian ethical framework*. The divergence between these theories, essentially, is the locus from which identity is developed; that is, does identity originate from one's own behavior and become adapted in relation to the greater culture and social norms, or does identity originate from greater social and cultural pressures and, in turn, shape one's personal behaviors?

The possible selves theory was proffered by Hazel Markus and Paula Nurius in the 1980s as an attempt to understand how people undergo changes in their lives that cut directly to their sense of self and personal identities. They state:

> Possible selves derive from representations of the self in the past and they include representations of the self in the future. They are different and separable from the current now selves, yet are intimately connected to them. . . . These possible selves are individualized and personalized, but they are also distinctly social. Many of these possible selves are the direct result of previous social comparisons in which the individual's own thoughts, feelings, characteristics, and behaviors have been contrasted to those of salient others.[10]

Essentially, this theory posits that the identity is created out of one's understanding of one's own behaviors, and how these behaviors relate to the culture at large. These possible selves, then, serve three main functions. First, they provide interpretive frameworks, which allows an individual to make sense of past behavior, providing a sort of comparative "means-ends" pattern for new behavior. For example, an individual who seeks to be a doctor will strive to do well in high school in order to increase the chances of admission to a reputable college, thus preparing him or her for medical school entrance.

Second, they provide additional meanings for current behavior based on a "context for possibility." For example, the student who is seeking to be a doctor will value a high grade in an organic chemistry or human anatomy class more so than a student who is seeking to be an accountant or lawyer.

Third, they provide a context for future behavior, as well as the viability and attainability of the possible self. For example, if a student who is seeking to be a doctor gets a failing grade in organic chemistry or human anatomy, this information can be used to either adjust the amount of effort needed for future similar courses, or reassess the attainability of becoming a doctor based on the performance.

In an interesting study that tested the role that the possible selves theory may play in preservice educators as compared to in-service educators, each set of participants were asked to describe versions of possible selves, and answers were compared. It was found that new in-service teachers reported versions of possible selves that were essentially "quality-focused," emphasizing elements such as the ability to connect with parents or students. Preservice teachers, however, reported versions of possible selves that were "task-focused," emphasizing elements such as finding a job and writing lesson plans on time.

These differences in findings indicate that the immediate environment has a strong influence on the conceptualization and formation of the possible self. That is, teachers who already have a job need not worry about finding one, but rather maintaining it by being a "quality" teacher, while preservice teachers have not yet secured their job, so are thinking more in these terms.[11]

The Foucauldian ethical framework attempts to apply some of the philosophical underpinnings of philosopher Michel Foucault's thought to the role

PRACTICE: DOES THE THEORY WORK IN REALITY?

Mr. M, a fifth-grade teacher in an urban school, has a friend who is a college professor in a teacher education program at a local university. They often talk about education, but he insists that his friend is too hung up on theory and is out of touch with actual practice. His friend, however, suggests that theory and practice are not as separate as Mr. M claims, and he could become a better teacher by learning more about theory.

1. Do you think that your identity originates in yourself and is shaped by the greater culture (à la *possible selves*) or do you believe that your identity originates in the greater culture and is shaped by your own interpretations (à la Foucault)?
2. Try to think of one or two classroom practices (or means of engagement with your students) that reflect this idea of origination.
3. Play with both theories. How do they fit into your growing professional identity?
   a. Try to devise one or two versions of a teacher "possible self." What does that "possible self" possess that your "current self" does not? Why does your "current self" not possess it? What is stopping your "current self" from being the "possible self"?
   b. Try to work out your personal conceptualizations of Foucault's four elements. How would you frame your *ethical substance*, your *mode of subjection*, your *forms of elaboration*, and your *telos*?
   c. Try to work each of these into your current practice as a teacher. What is already at play? What is not? Should it be?

of educators directly. Forwarded by Richard Niesche and Malcolm Haase,[12] this framework for identity development posits that what becomes the self is not invented by the individual, but rather is formed in response to society, culture, and social group practices as the combined result of four main processes. This framework is composed of four main components: (a) ethical substance; (b) mode of subjection; (c) forms of elaboration; and (d) telos.

Ethical substance is "the way in which the individual has to constitute this or that part of himself [or herself] as the prime material of moral conduct"[13] or what is involved in making ethical judgments. *Mode of subjection* is "the way in which the individual established his relation to the rule and recognizes him [or herself] as obliged to put it into practice"[14] or how people recognize their own moral obligations.

Forms of elaboration is "the ethical framework that one performs on oneself . . . to attempt to transform oneself into the ethical subject of one's behavior"[15] or how one "trains" in acting in respective moral manners. *Telos* is "an action that is not only moral in itself . . . [but is] . . . also moral in its circumstantial integration and . . . the place it occupies in a pattern of conduct,"[16] or the achievement of actually engaging in the sought-after moral behavior.

NOTES

1. https://www.huffpost.com/entry/mindfulness_b_4882114.
2. Janet Alsup. (2004). "Am I a Teacher? Exploring the Development of Professional Identity." *Language Arts Journal of Michigan*, *20*(1).
3. Catherine Beauchamp & L. Thomas. (2009). "Understanding Teacher Identity: An Overview of Issues in the Literature and Implications for Teacher Education." *Cambridge Journal of Education*, *39*(2), 175–189.
4. J. Sachs. (2005). "Teacher Education and Development of Professional Identity: Learning to be a Teacher." In P. Denicolo & M. Kompf (Eds.), *Connecting Policy and Practice: Challenges for Teaching and Learning in Schools and Universities* (pp. 5–21). Oxford: Routledge.
5. M. Frank Pajares. (1992). "Teachers' Beliefs and Educational Research: Cleaning Up a Messy Construct." *Review of Educational Research*, *62*(3), 307–332.
6. Virginia Richardson. (1996). "The Role of Attitude and Belief in Learning to Teach." In J. Sikula, T. J. Buttery, & E. Guyton (Eds.), *Handbook of Research on Teacher Education*. New York: Simon & Schuster Macmillan.
7. Pajares, 1992, p. 316.
8. Andy Hargreaves. (2001). "The Emotional Geographies of Teaching." *Teachers College Record*, *103*(6), 1056–1080.
9. Michalinos Zembylas. (2003). "Emotions and Teacher Identity: A Poststructural Perspective." *Teachers and Teaching: Theory and Practice*, *9*(3), 214–238.

10. Hazel Markus & P. Nurius. (1986). "Possible Selves." *American Psychologist*, *41*(9), 954–969.

11. Doug Hamman, K. Gosselin, & J. Romano et al. (2010). "Using Possible Selves Theory to Understand the Identity Development of New Teachers." *Teaching and Teacher Education*, *26*, 1349–1361.

12. Richard Niesche & M. Haase. (2012). Emotions and Ethics: A Foucauldian Framework for Becoming an Ethical Educator. *Educational Philosophy and Theory*, *44*(3), 276–288.

13. Michel Foucault. (1992). *The Use of Pleasure: A History of Sexuality*, *Vol II*. London, UK: Harmondsworth, Penguin, p. 26.

14. *Ibid.*, p. 27.

15. *Ibid.*

16. *Ibid.*

Chapter Three

The Stories We Tell

Narratives and the Formation of Our Identities

> "Belonging to a people is a precious thing. Maintaining that peoplehood requires discipline and sacrifice. Each group draws its boundaries differently—but no less sincerely."[1]
>
> —Merle and Phyllis Good

Narratives, or stories told to us that we then retell to others in words and actions, are a central component to cultural formation. Beyond simply hearing and telling these stories, however, we use these stories essentially as manuals on how we should live our lives, be it how we interact with others; how we receive or reject ideas; how and what we dress like, eat, speak like; and so on.

These narratives are essential in becoming who we are as part of a greater community, people, or culture. Julian Rappaport, a community psychologist, suggests that group narratives can be characterized in two distinct ways: community narratives and dominant cultural narratives.[2]

Community narratives are stories that are common among a particular group of people. These stories typically characterize or provide interpretation for that community's experience in the larger culture or society. Essential elements of the community's identity, such as their sense of history, development, contribution, and values, are transmitted through these narratives in both literal and symbolic manners such as social interactions, performances, works of art, and cultural rituals.

An example in American culture is "pride parades," which have become a common form of performance among communities that have experienced marginalization by the dominant culture, for which there is also often expressed opposition based on another community's conflicting narrative.

Dominant cultural narratives are stories that are pervasive within all aspects of a culture, including its subcultures, and act as a common "reference." These are the overarching cultural storylines that are maintained through influential social institutions such as mass media productions, religious institutions, political and civic agencies, and public schools.

For example, one of the strongest components of the American dominant cultural narrative is the notion of "liberty and justice for all," which is purported to overarch all elements of American society, touting the functionality of a "meritocracy" (success of the hardworking) over an "aristocracy" (success of the well-born), allowing everyone equal access to all that America has to offer.

There is, then, a reciprocal, responsive, and reactive interaction between these two main types of narratives in which the community narrative receives, reinterprets, and revises the way in which the messages of the dominant cultural narrative affect their community and, if the response is large enough, the dominant cultural narrative responds, reinterprets, and revises in turn. An example in American culture is the functionality of Black History Month (and, by extension, other "celebratory" months), whereas on the one hand these time periods can be used to honor groups that are otherwise marginalized in the dominant American narrative, therefore seen as an affirmative ritual.

PRACTICE: WHERE DO YOU BELONG?

Ms. K always had a very large and close Italian family. They ate dinner together almost every Sunday, and missing it was seen as a serious transgression. When she got married, her wife, whose heritage was different, did not have a large family and spoke with her mother and sister only once in a while. While they tried to maintain the Sunday dinner tradition, it was difficult for Ms. K's wife to feel comfortable, and eventually they stopped going regularly.

1. If you had to name the two most important communities in your life of which you are a part, what would they be?
2. Why did you choose these two communities specifically over other ones of which you may be a part? What is it about them, and your membership in them, that makes them so important?
3. If you had to identify two values of each community you chose, what would they be? Are they different from one another, or are they the same values?
4. Try to think of two ways in which you enact those values in your teaching practice.

The counternarrative, however, may claim that instead of setting aside "special" time frames in which to honor such groups, their cultural stories should be interwoven into the greater dominant narrative and, by extension, the mainstream curriculum, making special "honorary" periods obsolete.[3,4]

But exactly how these narratives serve to form culture and the interactions between people that take place within their boundaries remain useless if culture itself is not also defined. While the concept is most certainly evasive and inviting of multiple means of interpretation, culture can be regarded, at least for the purpose of this discussion, as "symbolic systems of embodied meaning by which people understand their experience of the world and in turn act upon it."[5]

Therefore, culture is itself defined as symbolic systems of embodied meaning that are transmitted by narratives and leads to the means by which individuals understand these meanings and act upon them. The narratives themselves, then, appear to be the source of cultural transmission, and the means by which we, as individuals, form our sense of cultural belonging and, by extension, our modes of living and interacting in our environment. The narrative by which we live and to which we contribute is therefore the source of both our cultural identity and our personal identity.

COMMUNITY NARRATIVES AS COMMUNICATION

Perhaps the most important element of cultural transmission is communication; that is, how we as people transmit the messages that we wish to share with other people. While likely regarded as obvious, the way in which an individual or community communicates is often indicative of the cultural values of that group itself. These differences in communication styles may become obvious when members of different communities begin to interact. As communication can be multifaceted and complicated, it is important to understand that communication involves more than just spoken or written language.

Images such as photographs, drawings, and paintings are powerful indicators of a community's message and communication style, which often can only be understood through an examination of the time and place in which such images were created, and by whom they were created. For example, in Buddhist temples colorful works of art, known as thangkas, convey deep messages about spiritual practices.

Objects such as religious relics, sculpture, and handiwork embody deep meanings about cultural values and can often be interpreted even more deeply by their specific placement in homes (displayed in a main room or private setting), their availability to others (whether they can be procured easily), and their level of protection (whether they are encased or in the open). All suggest the cultural meaning and value behind these objects. In a Jewish temple the Torah, or sacred scroll containing the Hebrew words of the Old Testament, remains closed and protected in an ark, or sacred box central to the altar, only to be taken out at certain times and touched by certain people.

Pierre Bourdieu, a French intellectual, was pivotal in studying and theorizing about the cultural context of communication. Through his concept of "social sedimentation," Bourdieu suggested that communication is self-building and reflects directly the focuses of a particular community at a particular time. As the community changes, the communication styles, as well as the content, change with it, adding a layer to the already established communication paradigm that came before it.

It is through this sedimentation process that the dominant cultural narrative is slowly replaced by a counternarrative (typically at the community level), which then re-sediments with a revised version of the dominant cultural narrative. This process continues ad infinitum, demonstrating the notion that the very culture is the narrative in process. Sediments can be composed of changes in generations, changes in political power, changes in religious influence, or any other significant social catalyst.[6]

Therefore, Bourdieu emphasized the cultural context of communication as it contributes to the *use* of language. For Bourdieu, language must only be considered as practical rather than grammatical, in that the grammar itself is also indicative of the community and its communicative purposes. That is, communication indicates one's individuality as well as one's cohesion with others in his or her affiliated groups, and the likenesses and differences between one's communication in comparison with one's affiliated groups are equally meaningful.[7] Considering slang in any community is indicative of this idea.

In most cases slang is used in social situations while grammatical English is used in formal situations. However, if one uses slang in a formal situation, a resulting cultural message is being conveyed, especially if it is used deliberately and purposefully. The notion of "code-switching" between cultures in the American professional environment is a good example of this notion in practice. The deep cultural context of communication, as well as the differences revealed by its juxtaposed nuances, is expressed by Dell Hymes, a well-known sociolinguist:

> Communities differ significantly in the ways of speaking, in patterns of repertoire and switching, in the roles and meanings of speech. They indicate differences with regard to beliefs, values, reference groups, norms, and the like . . . [differences which] . . . leap out when juxtaposed as contrasts that require explanation.[8]

COMMUNITY NARRATIVES AS TRANSMISSION OF TRUTH

What is clear is that one's sense of morality, civic duty, and citizenship is largely learned via cultural narratives. Its meanings, however, that is, how one is to apply these messages and conceptualize "truth," or what one can rely on as existent, are also embedded and transmitted through these cultural narratives. While there are multiple means by which these truths are transmitted, such as media, religious institutions, and familial interaction, the classroom is perhaps one of the most common places within which notions of cultural truth are both conveyed and reinforced. As Toshie Imada eloquently conveys:

> Formal education's most obvious function is to teach academic knowledge and skills. However, its other important function is to educate children to be proper members of the society with distinct cultural values . . . cultural norms, values and beliefs are transmitted rather implicitly, known as the "hidden curriculum."[9]

Indeed, while school is often regarded as an innocuous institution within which children may "practice" their skills for their future role in society, many educational scholars suggest that, on the contrary, it is within the classroom itself that society is being created and recreated, adding to the "sediment" of the current school-age generation.

The story becomes far more complicated when one is dealing with a plurality of cultures within a shared space. When this happens, what message or cultural norms should be, or will be, maintained when there are multiple, or even competing, conceptions of values, morals, and cultural narratives seen as most important by members of that culture?

The obvious answer may be that appealing to a feeling of empathy by discussing not only academic but also emotional content is what would transmit such experiential learning. However, this is only part of the story. What is equally important is emphasizing the continuity and cross-cultural applicability of the cultural effects of social and cultural events in history.

A telling study by John Wills explored the outcomes of teaching predominantly white children about slavery. Rather than engaging the children in the historical and persistent struggles involving race and racism, the transmission of the "story" resulted in the children perceiving slavery as more of a historical "snapshot," the sociopolitical results of which ended with the abolition of slavery.[10] As Wills writes:

> The reading or use of cultural texts (broadly defined) is not a simple process involving the transmission and consumption of meaning that is located "in" the text. It is rather a social and cultural process involving the fabrication or

PRACTICE: WHAT IS YOUR TRUTH?

While most of us would suggest that we are open-minded and accepting, we still have our deeply held truths that overarch our sense of civic obligation and responsibility. Let's explore these.

1. Try to give an example of a "truth"; that is, something that absolutely exists to you.
2. How might someone challenge that truth in one way or another?
3. Think of a historical event that would be considered tragic and place yourself as someone who experienced it directly. Write a diary entry to convey the authentic experience.

> construction of textual meaning, meaning that is not located in the text but in the interaction between cultural texts and their readers.[11]

In this we, as teachers, are implored not only to provide modes of transmitting information or even social and cultural meaning. Rather, we are further compelled to lead our students toward ways in which they can personally experience the effects of others' cultural narratives, allowing the "stories" to not only be mere tales, but rather real-life narrations as to what transpired before, and what may transpire again should we, as a culture, forget our past collective mistakes.

PERSONAL NARRATIVES AND THE CREATION OF ONE'S "SELF"

Community narratives are deeply important in allowing one to begin to form a foundation for one's own belief system, a sense of morals and values, and a sense of belonging to something larger than the individual. However, it would be erroneous to say that an individual is simply a reflection of his or her community and the embodiment of its narrative. Indeed, we all differ from our community's identity in one way or another, sometimes only slightly, sometimes quite significantly. It is these individualized versions of our social and cultural structure that can be called personal narratives. As Robyn Fivush et al. suggest:

> From the moment an individual is born, modern cultures reinforce the importance of having and telling one's story. . . . As early as 16 months of age . . .

> parents are already beginning to scaffold their child's ability to narrate their past by asking and elaborating on questions about what happened . . . "Did we have fun at the park today? . . . Did we go on the swings? . . . Yes, and didn't we swing high?"[12]

Developing personal narratives, then, allows the individual to find ways to perceive and interpret their society, culture, and immediate influences, and translate and develop these perceptions and interpretations into an overarching worldview. It is essential to remember, however, that the development of one's personal narrative is a direct outgrowth of the community narrative the individual has been receiving and interpreting for his or her entire life, even before the ability to verbalize one's observations and thoughts was acquired. As Julian Rappaport reminds us:

> Our personal life stories, idiosyncratic though they may be, are not formed whole cloth out of our individual choices. Personal life stories are negotiated in the context of narratives told by the communities in which we live. . . . Understanding community narratives is a way to understand culture and context and its profound effects on individual lives.[13]

One element that appears to be key in the identity formation process is that of autobiographical memory. Autobiographical memory extends one's ability to simply recall the basic "who, what, when, and where" of particular events, but also what these events meant, have come to mean, and why they were important enough to interpret so deeply. They comprise the story of an individual's life in the context of emotions, relationships, intentions, and motivations, all of which contributes to the formation of a sense of self, including the culturally valued ways of expressing oneself and contextualizing one's story.[14]

To reference Imada's aforementioned ideas, in an individualistic society such as that of America, cultural referents to winning or achieving are often reinforced in children's interactions (such as winning sports tournaments, academic competitions, or college admission), whereas in a more collectivistic society such as that of Japan, cultural referents to conformity or group harmony are reinforced (such as reaching a consensus about an issue in a class or determining how one's personal role benefited the larger community).

As with other elements involved in the identity formation process, autobiographical memory is developed by multiple related subcomponents that are enacted from the very beginning of one's life, even before the individual can talk. These subcomponents include basic memory systems (such as recall and naming); acquisition of complex signed or spoken language; production and comprehension of narrative components such as plot, characters, and theme;

PRACTICE: BEGINNING TO TELL YOUR STORY

1. Name two essential elements to your "life story." That is, if you were given a chance to tell it, what would *have to* be included in order for it to be complete?
2. Now consider how these two essential elements have been influenced by your culture (however you choose to define or contextualize it). In what ways are they culturally specific or culturally dependent?
3. If you came to live among another culture, would you be able to explain it in the same way, or would the context have to be made clearer?
4. Unpack it a bit. In what ways are the elements of autobiographical memory at work here? How do these memories specifically relate to your emotions, relationships, and interpretations of those either directly or indirectly involved?

style of parent talk; personal perspective; attribution of one's own and others' mental states; and psychological understanding.[15]

As these develop in complexity and application, one is able to combine them to initiate and refine one's autobiographical memories, and contextualize them within one's own personal narrative.

It becomes clear, then, that while personal narratives are, indeed, representations of the way in which individuals perceive and interpret their culture and surroundings in context, the personal narrative is quite literally dependent on the community narrative. Therefore, developing one's teacher identity must follow the same course. As has been established, schooling, and the social, cultural, and historical narrative one learns in schools, is by no means culturally agnostic; rather, it is perhaps the most distilled form of cultural transmission that exists.

Essentially, the school curriculum is designed to encompass all the social and cultural rules, ideas, and ideals that one must believe in order to be a part of that culture's system. As Jefferson Singer suggests:

> To understand the identity formation process is to understand how individuals craft narratives from experiences, tell these stories internally and to others, and ultimately apply these stories to knowledge of self, other, and the world in general.[16]

But what must teachers consider when trying to apply the identity formation process to their teaching lives, or their identity *as* teachers? Spending time and effort attending to the development of a teacher identity, or what will be referred to as a "teacher self," continues to receive much attention. As Catherine Beauchamp and Lynn Thomas posit:

> Student teachers must undergo a shift in identity as they move through programs of teacher education and assume positions as teachers in today's challenging school contexts. In addition, further identity shifts may occur throughout a teacher's career as a result of interactions within schools and in broader communities.[17]

The identity formation process, therefore, is not only important but also automatic and perpetual. That is, it will happen, and continue to happen, even without one's attention to it. However, if a teacher attends to it consistently through reflection, the formation process will be significantly more deep, directed, and genuine.

Rather than proposing a specific definition for teacher identity, however, which always risks deep and detracting subjectivity and bias, the theoretical framework for "personal growth" proposed by scholars Jack Bauer and Dan McAdams will be applied.[18] According to these scholars, personal growth encompasses four main themes: integrative, intrinsic, agentic, and communal. Each of these elements contributes a specialized process in the development of identity, with the common understanding that all development in identity can, and should, be considered growth regardless of its immediate effect.

PRACTICE: BEGINNING YOUR "PROCESSES"

Mr. M grew up in a small town in a very religious and politically conservative family. Issues such as homosexuality, drugs and alcohol, and anything deemed "liberal" were avoided, if not forbidden in conversation. Once Mr. M began to attend college at a large university in a city a few states away, he became exposed to people of different races, religions, and lifestyles. His roommate was gay, and his roommate's boyfriend was Hispanic. He also took a women's studies course in which he met a black lesbian, as well as a Jewish woman who identified as bisexual.

1. Try to think of a way in which you engaged in integrative processes. When you encountered an opposing view, did you ever change your mind or deepen your existing belief?
2. Now try to think of how this integrative process contributed to an intrinsic process. That is, how did this "change" affect you emotionally?
3. Finally, was there an agentic and/or communal effect? If so, what was it? If not, why do you think it did not reach that stage of growth?

Integrative processes, regarded as social-cognitive, involve the way in which one differentiates and incorporates new and different views of self and others. This may refer to the idea of changing one's mind or developing deeper understandings of a preserved belief or perception. Integrative processes have a widening effect, allowing the individual to act in a growing range of situations. Intrinsic processes, regarded as social-emotional, involve the incorporation of stimuli that directly affect one's happiness, meaningfulness of relationships, and quality of one's contribution to society.

Typically, intrinsic processes revolve around emotional elements of motivation (pride, sense of contribution, justice) as opposed to material ones (money, tangible recognition, promotion). Both processes contribute to one's agentic growth, or the ability to impact one's environment or fulfillment of personal goals, as well as communal growth, or enhancing and deepening one's meaningful connection and contribution to social groups that exist beyond oneself.

THE EMOTIONAL SELF

The role of emotion is a central component of the conversation on teacher identity. Emotion is a base human process and is, essentially, unavoidable, and plays an integral role in any human interaction. Indeed, as Beauchamp and Thomas suggest, "[e]motion may alter a teacher's identity in relation to the profession, but may also be altered by aspects of the profession."[19]

Therefore, not only is emotion unavoidable in a professional context, it is reciprocal, both being informed by and informing the "self" that is in action in that context. On a daily basis teachers will encounter elements of the practice that affect their emotion, including the role of caring, the emotions of their children, interpersonal professional interactions, and practical implications of sweeping education reform (such as was seen in the case of the Common Core State Standards).

Zembylas identifies emotions as "part of the very fabric constituting the self, but are socially managed through social conventions, community scrutiny, legal norms, familial obligations, and religious injunctions."[20] In this context, emotion is a central factor in the identification of the self, but is heavily mediated by external cultural factors.

While one cannot prevent emotion from occurring, one must also consider the social and cultural context for which that emotion can and should be expressed. Further, Zembylas suggests that emotion itself must be more deeply understood before its role in the development of professional identity can be truly considered.

First, emotions are contextualized within language and are references to a wider social life, rather than being a "passive process" that happens to "sufferers." From this view, the distinction between the private and the public domains of emotions is blurred. Notions and positions of power are inherent in language used about emotion, especially in the context of what emotions one can express, as well as how and to whom, such as emotion being used as a means of social and political resistances. Finally, the role of the body must also be considered in both the feeling and the expression of emotions, challenging the notion that they are, essentially, a psychological phenomenon, but also a physiological one.[21]

But is it just that emotions play a role in our teaching lives, or is the job of teaching an inherently emotional process, or what Hochschild calls "emotional labor"?[22] More than this, however, is the overarching notion in Western culture that there is a definitive boundary between "thinking" and "feeling,"

PRACTICE: INTERACTIONS AND EMOTIONS IN TEACHER IDENTITY

Ms. K recently accepted a job in an urban school that had a reputation of being "rough." Her class was split nearly evenly between black students and Hispanic students who were mostly Ecuadoran, but some Puerto Rican. Having difficulty connecting with them, one day she tried to learn about their different cultures by spending some time asking questions. After receiving no responses, one student finally said, "Why do you care, anyway? You're just going to leave for a better job in a white school as soon as you can anyway, just like everybody else."

1. Think about an interaction you've had with a student, colleague, or supervisor that "jarred" your sense of "identity." Describe the situation, and then explore what about the interaction was significant.
2. Let's focus on emotion specifically. What are your thoughts about the expression of emotion in a teaching context? What are the limitations, and why might they exist?
3. In what way do you think you display your emotions "physiologically"? How might this affect a communication partner? Do you have any experiences with this?
4. How did you come to form your beliefs about the expression of emotion? Where did the "rules" come from?
5. How have you handled intense or difficult emotions in the classroom yourself?

relegating feeling to be bereft of thought, and thought bereft of feeling. As Kenneth Zeichner and Daniel Liston suggest:

> There seems to be a cultural and professional reluctance about combining reflective teaching and reflective feeling. This reluctance seems to grow out of a strong and resilient norm against commingling thinking (reasoning) and feeling (emotions) . . . there seems to be an abiding view that emotion and reason are either opposed to each other or that reason serves to control the untoward outbreaks of emotion.[23]

The general message, then, is to distinguish between the distraction of emotion and the progress of reason. This notion is woven deeply into the fabric of the Western sense of professionalism. Indeed, in professional culture there exist a number of aphorisms that contribute to this distinction that we, as "workers," often learn quickly, with some banal, such as "check your baggage at the door," and some more admonishing, such as "don't dip your pen in company ink."

Despite the specificity of confusing your personal problems with your professional ones or risking investing emotion into a romantic relationship with someone at work, the idea is clear: emotion of any kind is antithetical to professionalism.

NOTES

1. Merle Good & P. Good. (2001). *20 Most Asked Questions about the Amish and Mennonites*. New York: Simon & Schuster.
2. Julian Rappaport. (2000). "Community Narratives: Tales of Terror and Joy." *American Journal of Community Psychology*, *28*(1), 1–24.
3. LaGarrett J. King & K. Brown. (2014). "Once a Year to Be Black: Fighting Against Typical Black History Month Pedagogies." *Negro Educational Review*, *65*, 23–43.
4. John H. Franklin, G. Horne, H. Cruse, A. Ballard, & R. Mitchell, Jr. (1997). "Black History Month: Serious Truth Telling or a Triumph in Tokenism." *Journal of Blacks in Higher Education*, *18*, 87–92.
5. Anne Kane. (2000). "Reconstructing Culture in Historical Explanation: Narrative as Cultural Structure and Practice." *History and Theory*, *39*, 311–330.
6. Sean Phelan. (2011). "The Media as Neoliberalized Sediment: Articulating Laclau's Discourse Theory with Bourdieu's Field Theory." In Lincoln Dahlberg and S. Phelan (Eds.), *Discourse Theory and Cultural Media Politics* (pp. 128–153). New York: Springer.
7. Iffat Farah. (1998). "The Ethnography of Communication." In N. H. Horenberger and P. Corson (Eds.), *Encyclopedia of Language and Education: Volume*

8: Research Methods in Language and Communication (pp. 125–133). Dordrecht, Netherlands: Kluwer.

8. Dell Hymes. (1972). "Models of Interactions of Language and Social Life." In J. Gumperz & D. Hymes (Eds.), *Directions in Sociolinguistics: The Ethnography of Communication* (pp. 35–71). Oxford: Blackwell.

9. Toshie Imada. (2012). "Cultural Narratives of Individualism and Collectivism: A Content Analysis of Textbook Stories in the United States and Japan." *Journal of Cross-Cultural Psychology*, *43*(4), 576–591.

10. John S. Wills. (1996). "Who Needs Multicultural Education? White Students, US History, and the Construction of a Usable Past." *Anthropology & Education Quarterly*, *27*(3), 365–389.

11. John S. Wills. (1994). "Popular Culture, Curriculum, and Historical Representation: The Situation of Native Americans in History and the Perpetuation of Stereotypes." *Journal of Narrative and Life History*, *4*(4), 277–294.

12. Robyn Fivush, T. Habermas, T. E. A. Waters, et al. (2011). "The Making of Autobiographical Memory: Intersections of Culture, Narrative, and Identity." *International Journal of Psychology*, *46*(5), 321–345.

13. Julian Rappaport. (2000). "Community Narratives: Tales of Terror and Joy." *American Journal of Community Psychology*, *28*(1), 1–24.

14. Fivush et al., 2011.

15. Katherine Nelson & R. Fivush. (2004). "The Emergence of Autobiographical Memory: A Social Cultural Developmental Theory." *Psychological Review*, *111*(2), 486–511.

16. Jefferson A. Singer. (2004). "Narrative Identity and Meaning Making across the Adult Lifespan: An Introduction." *Journal of Personality*, *72*(3), 437–459.

17. Catherine Beauchamp & L. Thomas. (2009). "Understanding Teacher Identity: An Overview of Issues in the Literature and Implications for Teacher Education." *Cambridge Journal of Education, 39*(2), 175–189.

18. Jack Bauer & D. McAdams. (2004). "Personal Growth in Adults' Stories of Life Transitions." *Journal of Personality*, *72*(3), 573–602.

19. Beauchamp &Thomas, 2004, p. 180.

20. Michalinos Zembylas. (2003). "Interrogating 'Teacher Identity': Emotion, Resistance, and Self-Formation." *Educational Theory*, *53*(1), 107–127.

21. *Ibid.*

22. Arlie Hochschild. (1983). *The Managed Heart*. Berkeley: University of California Press.

23. Zeichner & Liston, 2014, p. 39.

Chapter Four

The Space between Us

Teachers, Administrators, and Creating a Culture of Reflection

"Politics is the dirty foam on the surface of the river, while the life of the river is lived much deeper."[1]

—Milan Kundera, *The Unbearable Lightness of Being*

The place and role of the administrator is a precarious and contested one among teachers. The involvement of an administrator can, at its best, be highly supportive, constructive, and productive, or at its worst, deeply detrimental and dysfunctional. Educational administration, however, has become a permanent and ever more present fixture in the educational landscape, and its permanence necessitates a closer exploration of the teacher-administrator relationship, especially as it relates to creating a culture of reflection.

Essentially, it is the administration that determines whether the school culture is a safe and shared one in which reflection, discussion, and self-examination, as well as their inherent risks, are encouraged and nourished, or a fearful and political one in which rules and policy are simply enforced as dictated by the powerful.

ADMINISTRATORS AS CULTURAL LEADERS

In the current climate of school reform, accountability of multiple types has taken the forefront of policy discussion and implementation. While much of the pressure has been focused on teachers in the form of student test scores, it is important to recognize that the pressure placed upon administrators, specifically building-level administrators such as principals, has also been unduly increasing. With this increase in pressure comes also an increasing complexity in role, with principals being expected to serve leadership roles in educational, managerial, and political capacities.[2]

As school leaders, administrators are, perhaps, the most crucial in both preserving and changing the culture of the school in which they serve. In this context, school culture is best represented using Edgar Schein's (1992) conceptualization as having three main parts: (a) artifacts, such as the building design, physical displays, rituals, and educational traditions; (b) values, such as competition or collaboration, inclusivity or hierarchy, which govern, both explicitly and tacitly, the behavior of the organization's members; and (c) assumptions, such as the underlying perceptions of "reality" and "space," in which the culture perpetuates itself.[3]

This idea is put best by Kent D. Peterson and T. E. Deal:

> Strong and positive cultures do not just happen. They are built over time by those who work in and attend the school and by formal and informal leaders who encourage and reinforce values and traditions. . . . Leaders must shape and nourish cultures where teachers can make a difference and every child can learn and where there is a passion and commitment to designing and promoting the absolutely best that is possible.[4]

Indeed, the responsibility of building-level administrators is disproportionate in heft, as it falls on a single individual. However, this is a current reality and the implicit obligation accepted by the administrator. What then must the administrator do in order to preserve the elements of the culture that are sacred and effective as well as change those that are not? Fostering a culture of reflection is a key factor in achieving such a goal. It is important to note that specific elements of a positive school culture will not be explored or suggested. Indeed, that is not the purpose. Rather, how the members of a school community, under the leadership of the administration, can reflect effectively upon their own needs, wants, and goals and determine such elements will be emphasized.

A main element of being a cultural leader is the commitment to engage in continuous professional development oneself. Leaders of cultural development cannot be effective if their perspective remains unchallenged and stagnant. Administrators who engage regularly in professional development activities not only foster their own growth as leaders, but also the growth of the teachers and students in their school.[5]

The ability to both engage in meaningful professional development and enact such changes is persistently hampered by a seemingly relentless influx of managerial demands such as student and teacher disciplinary needs, parent concerns, staffing challenges, and the like, necessitating a version of an administrator that is essentially a thinly stretched multitasker "putting out fires" continuously rather than a stable leader able to effect real change.[6] It is for this reason that the centrality of professional development and cultural work needs to be both recognized and planned for by central administration, and that building administrators be provided the genuine opportunity to engage in such important work.

In order for such professional development to take place, and for the outcomes of the development to firmly take root in the school culture, there must be an increase in recognition of the importance of professional development in the school culture in general, including the teachers, students, parents, and all facets of administrators. Professional development can often be regarded as "days off" or "running out the clock" situations in which little knowledge is actually gained and the time is scarcely spent constructively.

It is for this reason that professional development itself must take on a reflective form. That is, provision of professional development for all educational stakeholders should not be haphazardly determined from a "top-down" perspective, but rather from a collective one. Allowing those who receive the professional development to determine themselves what they would value is imperative for cultural improvement in two main ways. First, it requires the receivers of the professional development to explore and evaluate their own needs, which is a vital form of reflection. Equally important, however, it allows

PRACTICE: BUILDING A CULTURE OF REFLECTION

After a particularly poor observation, Mr. B met with his principal, Dr. S, for a debriefing. During the meeting, Dr. S asked few questions. Rather, he listed a number of things that he thought Mr. B needed to do, and then assured him that he would be back to observe him again, and expected changes.

1. In what way, if any, do administrators seek the feedback of teachers when determining what professional development topics will be provided? What might this say about the "structure" of the administration in your school?
2. Explore the following:
   a. If you are a teacher, what do you believe your building administrator's view of professional development is?
   b. If you are an administrator, how do you think the teachers in your school would characterize your view of professional development?
   c. Compare these answers, if you can.
3. Let's explore your school's culture. Identify two positive elements of the current culture in your school, and why you'd argue that they should be preserved. Now identify two negative elements of the current culture in your school, and why you'd argue that they should be corrected or changed.

the receivers to have agency over their own training and edification, providing for a form of shared governance and participatory decision-making.

Availability of meaningful professional development is a vital component in the pursuit of what has come to be called "authentic leadership." According to Paul Begley:

> Authentic leadership may be thought of as a metaphor for professionally effective, ethically sound, and consciously reflective practices in educational administration. [It] is knowledge-based, values informed, and skillfully executed . . . values are formally defined and proposed as an influence on the actions of individuals as well as on administrative practice. . . . [It] implies a genuine kind of leadership—a hopeful, open-ended, visionary, and creative response to social circumstances . . . [as opposed to] mechanistic, short-sighted, precedent-focused and context-constrained practices.[7]

Essentially, authentic leadership requires school administrators to balance and reinforce the development of personal, professional, organizational, and social values, and to foster the relationship between them toward an academically, emotionally, and socially supportive school culture. Authentic leadership should, therefore, be the main goal of administrators, especially those at the building level, with the focus on cultivating the culture of reflection.

CULTIVATING RELATIONSHIPS BETWEEN TEACHERS AND ADMINISTRATORS

While the word "relationship" and its related concepts have often had a place in the educational discourse, it has failed, in many ways, to become a live principle rather than a passive term. However, the nature and quality of the relationship between teachers and administrators have been demonstrated to be essential in cultivating a constructive and productive school culture. Elements of the school environment ranging from teacher learning and development to student achievement and everything in between appear to be related to the quality of the teacher-administrator relationship.

While there is no question that relationships are reciprocal, it is largely the responsibility of the administrator, as the school leader, to initiate the relationship, as well as maintain it, fostering the conceptualizations and outplay of essential institutional norms of collegiality, support, instruction, and feedback.[8]

An element of the complexity of defining and developing relationships is its multifaceted nature, creating difficulty as to which element should be fostered most. In the context of reflection, however, it is suggested that the element of support, specifically, a principal's support of teachers, is vital and deserving of attention first. Support can be characterized in terms of four domains: environmental, instructional, technical, and emotional, all of which play an integral role in the quality of the relationship between teachers and principals.[9]

Support appears to be so important that it can even be directly attributable to teacher retention, with perceived presence of support identified as incentive for retention and absence as impetus for attrition.[10] Specifically, areas of emotional support, specifically positive recognition and constructive feedback, as well as environmental support, such as providing materials, space, and staffing when necessary, appear to be most essential.[11]

Timing of relationships also appears to be distinctly important. While it is important for principals to have supportive relationships with all teachers, it is of utmost importance to establish such relationships with new teachers, either at the novice level or merely new within the building. While teachers who have been working in a building for an extended period of time have been familiarized with the culture and have had the opportunity to foster supportive relationships with their colleagues, novice teachers or teachers new to the building are particularly vulnerable due to their unfamiliarity with the field as a whole, the school in general, or both.

Principals, therefore, must make a distinct effort to provide support in both personal development, such as socialization of the new teacher, and professional development, such as instructional and academic growth as it relates

PRACTICE: THE RELATIONSHIP BETWEEN TEACHERS AND PRINCIPALS

Mrs. L is a new principal in a middle school that has a high turnover rate, mostly because it has the reputation of being "anti-teacher." As a result, her main goal is to establish a better relationship between teachers and administrators. She begins by having open-door office hours during teacher lunchtimes to encourage open conversation.

1. Try to come up with a definition for the word "relationship" as it specifically describes teachers and administrators (or principals in particular). Why might developing such a definition be important?
2. In what ways does your principal provide support in each area (environmental, instructional, technical, emotional)? In what ways is support lacking in these areas?
3. In which area do you believe support should be focused first and why?

to the school culture in particular. While efforts in this area are unmistakably present in schools, such as through mentor programs or mandatory probationary teacher meetings, such initiatives run the risk of becoming perfunctory, and therefore lacking any real effect on teaching practice and schoolwide culture. As such, it is incumbent upon the principal to facilitate the translation of such developmental activities to real cultural change.

Essentially, principal support can be distilled into one essential goal: developing teacher resiliency. This can be achieved through supporting a culture of reflection in which risk-taking is not only supported, but encouraged, and the outcome of such risks, no matter what they are, will be met with more support, encouragement, and reflection. Developing teacher resiliency, therefore, is a mode of nurturing teacher empowerment that, despite sounding like a threat to the political balance of the school, has been shown to be distinctly constructive.

FOSTERING TEACHER SELF-EFFICACY AND RESILIENCY

Self-efficacy is a term that is often "bandied about," and as a result it has gained a reputation as a fluffy and imprecise concept in the vein of "pop psychology" that is devoid of any real meaning. This is unfortunate, as self-efficacy is a highly important and predictive concept in the success of many facets of teaching. Initially developed by the psychologist Albert Bandura in the 1970s, self-efficacy is the belief in one's capability to organize and execute courses of action that are required to manage particular situations.[12]

It has been shown to be distinctly important in both teacher effectiveness and empowerment, as teachers who have a high sense of efficacy are more likely to be able to question, refine, and improve their instructional approaches without self-consciousness, as well as foster high self-efficacy among their students, who in turn achieve highly in a number of areas.

What is most important in this context is that reflective practice has been shown to be highly related to an increase in teacher self-efficacy, therefore leading to exponential positive development. That is, teachers who reflect are more self-efficacious; teachers who work in schools with principals that foster reflection are more apt to become self-efficacious, yielding more teachers who are more self-efficacious; schools with more self-efficacious teachers are apt to have more self-efficacious students and will therefore be more highly achieving.[13]

In addition to the advantage that cultivating self-efficacy has on school culture and student achievement, it has also been shown to be highly related to teacher retention. As demands increase and pressures magnify for teachers, students, and administrators alike, retention becomes more challenging. Complicating factors such as low pay, large class sizes, low levels of support, and student behavior challenges exacerbate this already precarious situation in the most vulnerable of schools.

While elements of school improvement that involve resources such as monetary budgets, instructional and technological materials, and support staff will ever be challenging, principal support of a reflective culture has no cost, and can only benefit the school culture as a whole. Moving toward a culture of collective self-efficacy will allow even the most challenged schools to maintain a positive sense of identity and pride, and be able to meet and answer challenges positively and collaboratively rather than destructively and disruptively and motivated by blame and resentment.[14]

Self-efficacy alone, however, does not complete the story of what benefits may come from supportive principal relationships. Another concept, known often as resiliency, also plays a central role in both longevity and effectiveness of a teacher, and is developed through reflective practice. Resiliency can be conceptualized as the ability of teachers to adjust to variable and potentially adverse situations while maintaining or increasing their competence.[15] Resiliency is influenced by multiple factors including self-esteem,

PRACTICE: TEACHER SELF-EFFICACY AND YOU

Mr. N regards himself as a technical teacher. He spends little time or effort fostering relationships with students since he is assessed not on how much he is liked, but on how well his students perform. Over the past three years Mr. N has grown frustrated, since he prides himself on knowing his content well, but his students have had low assessment scores overall. His initial thought is to raise the expectations for his students and require even more homework for content practice. He also limited student questions during class to avoid going off track.

1. Try to identify two or three teaching situations in which self-efficacy plays more of a role than academic or content knowledge. Explain a bit.
2. What are ways in which you have addressed your self-efficacy directly in an attempt to improve it? Share some strategies if possible.
3. Is self-efficacy a topic that has been discussed at professional development sessions or faculty meetings? Why or why not? What might this say about the role self-efficacy plays in your school's culture?
4. Do you believe, as a teacher, that you have developed a sense of resiliency? If so, what has helped you do so? If not, what has been the biggest barrier to such development?

self-efficacy, sense of motivation, resourcefulness, and physical, mental, and emotional health.[16]

To be resilient, teachers must be able to call upon their own resources, including past experience, education, and philosophy, as well as confidence in administrator support of their resulting instructional decisions. When a principal has reinforced teachers' expertise and autonomy and affirmed the teachers' trust in their support, teachers are able to act with greater confidence, and in the absence of hesitation due to uncertainty of their principal's potential response.

Because the teacher has faith in the principal's support, this faith acts as a "buffer" of sorts, allowing for professional risk-taking and confidence in trying novel approaches with students.[17] By making support of the reflective process a cornerstone of the teacher-principal relationship, teachers can continuously reflect upon their decisions and outcomes of the instructional risks taken, leading to more self-efficacy, greater confidence, more variety of instructional resources, and an ever-strengthening school culture.

NOTES

1. Milan Kundera. (2004). *The Unbearable Lightness of Being.* New York: Harper Row.
2. Bruce G. Barnett & G. R. O'Mahony. (2006). "Developing a Culture of Reflection: Implication for School Improvement." *Reflective Practice*, *7*(4), 499–523.
3. Schein, E. H. (1992). *Organizational Culture and Leadership*. San Francisco, Jossey-Bass. See also Barnett & O'Mahony, 2006, 499–523.
4. Kent D. Peterson & T. E. Deal. (2002). *The Shaping of School Culture Fieldbook.* San Francisco: Jossey-Bass.
5. Frances K. Kochan, P. Bredeson, & C. Riehl. "Rethinking Development of School Leaders." *Yearbook for the National Society of the Study of Education*, *101*(1), 289–306.
6. *Ibid.*
7. Paul T. Begley. (2003). "In Pursuit of Authentic School Leadership Practices." In Paul T. Begley & O. Johansson (Eds.), *The Ethical Dimensions of School Leadership* (pp. 1–12). Netherlands: Kluwer.
8. Richard Butt & J. Retalik. (2002). "Professional Well-Being and Learning: A Study of Administrator-Teacher Workplace Relationships." *Journal of Educational Enquiry*, *3*(1), 17–34.
9. Amy L. Hughes, J. J. Matt, & F. L. O'Reilly. (2015). "Principal Support Is Imperative to the Retention of Teachers in Hard-to-Staff Schools." *Journal of Education and Training Studies*, *3*(1), 129–134.

10. S. J. Otto & M. Arnold. (2005). "A Study of Experienced Special Education Teachers' Perceptions of Administrative Support." *College Student Journal*, *39*(2), 253–259.

11. Hughes et al., 2015.

12. Sheryl Y. Kennedy & J. B. Smith. (2013). "The Relationship Between School Collective Reflective Practice and Teacher Physiological Efficacy Sources." *Teaching and Teacher Education*, *29*, 132–143.

13. *Ibid.*

14. Deborah S. Yost. (2006). "Reflection and Self-Efficacy: Enhancing the Retention of Qualified Teachers from a Teacher Education Perspective." *Teacher Education Quarterly*, *33*(4), 59–76.

15. Becky L. Bobek. (2002). "Teacher Resiliency: A Key to Career Longevity." *The Clearing House*, *75*(4), 202–205.

16. Antonio J. Castro, J. Kelly, & M. Shih. (2010). "Resilience Strategies for New Teachers in High-Needs Areas." *Teaching and Teacher Education*, *22*, 622–629.

17. *Ibid.*

Chapter Five

The Necessity of Difference and Diversity

Pinning Down Cultural Bias

> "The closer one gets to realize one's destiny, the more that destiny becomes their true reason for being."[1]
>
> —Paulo Coelho, *The Alchemist*

The centrality of narratives—the stories one tells to oneself and to others—is central to the notion of cultural bias. While most of us would prefer to insist that we have no cultural bias, the dirty and regrettable truth is that we *all* do. The most important element in exploring what those biases are is disarming the notion of bias itself; to strip it of its power over us, and to recognize that once we realize the biases with which we approach the world, and by extension our classrooms, then and only then can we begin to dismantle them.

The basis of our thinking, what we believe as right and wrong, comes from our culture and various subcultures. The religion in which we are raised or choose to follow, the political ideologies we were taught or espouse, the philosophical traditions we accept or reject, all comprise the complexity of our personal "culture" and what we take and apply from it.

Therefore, the depth with which we explored our cultures earlier can now be used, in a deeper sense, to explore our biases. The more open and honest we are with ourselves in this context, the deeper we will be able to acknowledge and transform the biases that are functioning, likely tacitly, in the fibers of our lives and work.

Essentially, our work with our own biases becomes the most important, yet the most difficult and mentally challenging, element of reflective practice. This is the essence of the reflective mirror. We do not choose what gets reflected back to us, but we do choose what we do with it, and how openly and compassionately we accept the reality of its existence. Of the elements of the reflection we can change, we determine how best to do so, where to start, and what we wish to change into.

Of the elements we may not necessarily be able to change, at least readily, we recognize our complete control over how we incorporate them into our lives and work as it is, and as it will be. Therefore, balancing our need to change that which we can with our need to surrender mindfully to that which we cannot becomes the recipe for deep and effective reflection. This chapter will focus on those elements that we can, with earnest effort and honesty, change.

In order to participate in a reflection about cultural bias there are two imperatives. First, you must accept that you possess biases to begin with. That is, while we would all prefer to view ourselves as objective, fair, and unprejudiced, the fact is that we are not. Second, you must accept that your biases cause you to behave and act in certain ways toward certain types of people, often in a way that stems from or creates inequality.

As an actively reflective teacher, author, researcher, and community participant I have been forced to continually face my own biases and confront how these biases influence my thoughts, feelings, beliefs, writing, teaching, talking, as well as how they change, develop, and simply turn into different biases. Indeed, these biases are ever-present throughout the book, and will be in the context of this chapter as well.

This chapter will approach cultural bias in an inductive manner. That is, it will be suggested that cultural bias is the outcome of cultural narratives that are, essentially, the basis for teachers' classroom-based behaviors. These cultural narratives are themselves developed and maintained in a somewhat cyclical and perpetual fashion based on other concepts that are internal and external as well as social and personal. The main contributive concepts that will be explored in this chapter are *racism* (and by extension other forms of culturally based systematic exclusion such as nationalism, xenophobia, ethnocentrism, sexism, heterosexism, and ableism, among others), *hegemony, bigotry*, *colorblindness,* and *bias* (specifically cultural and confirmatory bias).

RACISM, HEGEMONY, BIGOTRY, AND COLORBLINDNESS

Racism, in many senses, has become one of the most misused, misapplied, and misunderstood concepts in the American sociopolitical and sociocultural dialogue. In public discourse, especially that handled by any facet of what can be considered mainstream media, the term "racism," or more aptly "racist," is often weaponized or leveled at someone in order to shame them or hold them responsible for some statement or action committed against someone of another race or ethnicity. In this context, racism, or being "racist," is confounded with bigotry, or being a "bigot." Gerardo Lopez, a racial educational policy scholar, helps us to understand the difference between these terms.

> Racism is perceived as an individual and irrational act in a world that is otherwise neutral, rational, and just . . . it positions racism at the individual level and ignores other ways in which it functions in society. Racism . . . has been reduced to broad generalizations about another group based on the color of their skin. It has become an individual construction as opposed to a social and/or civilizational construct . . . viewed as deviant behaviors and/or attitudes in an otherwise neutral world.[2]

Lopez's point and distinction are crucial. When people describe racism, they use the definition for what is more aptly bigotry. By doing this, people allow themselves to deny their own contribution to racism, as well as exonerate themselves from any acts that may be considered racist. Therefore, the conclusion that it is irrational and hateful people who engage in racism, and are therefore the real racists, is able to fit snugly into their personal narrative. The problem is that this conceptualization is patently false. When racism is properly defined in the broader sociological and systematic context of job distribution, residency discrimination, wage inequality, and the like, most in the "middle class" have no choice but to see themselves as a contributor to racism.

As an example from my own life, despite self-identifying as an antiracist scholar and educator, I contribute daily to the perpetuation of racism based on where I have decided to live with my family (a predominantly white suburban town) and work (a predominantly white private college) who enjoys the benefits of white privilege on a daily basis (including living essentially free of law enforcement presence, and in the rare case of its presence, I am more likely regarded as the protected rather than the aggressor). In this sense, because my daily existence in and of itself contributes to the perpetuation of racism, I can accurately be characterized as a "racist."

Therefore, racism, in this context, will be conceptualized as acts that contribute to the perpetuation of the systematic inequality in the availability of social, political, and economic mobility and capital resulting from one's race. Seemingly permanent social examples of racism from this perspective are demonstrated by comparing sentencing trends by race or ethnicity for comparable criminal offenses, employment opportunities for ex-convicts, job offers extended to people based on name alone, among other disparities.[3,4,5] By extension, cultural processes such as xenophobia, ethnocentrism, sexism, heterosexism, ableism, and others also refer to systematic oppression and marginalization of people based on identification with particular cultures, subcultures, lifestyles, and/or preferences.

As Lopez teaches us, the conflation of terms between racism and bigotry is not only precarious but serves a very important social function, especially for members of the dominant, or what is better characterized as the hegemonic, culture. The term *hegemonic* was likely popularized by Antonio Gramsci, an Italian antifascist intellectual from the first part of the 20th century. According to Gramsci's conceptualization, hegemony can be thought of as the dominant rule of one particular culture, as applies to political, social, and economic enterprises, whose main goal is to preserve its power either by consent of the people (tacit or explicit) or by force.

By preserving their power in both legislative and social arenas, members of the hegemonic culture also preserve their interests and maintain the ability to exert influence on virtually all cultural institutions including schools, religious organizations, media, political and governmental boards, and civic associations.[6] Essentially, the social permissibility of the hegemonic culture to remain the hegemonic culture is what allows racism, as well as other forms of systematic marginalization, to continue in a largely unchallenged, if not normalized, manner.

It is the hegemonic culture's ability to steer the cultural narrative that allows the definition of racism to continuously be obscured and conflated. *Bigotry* therefore can best be described as intentional acts of hate, aggression, or violence intended to hurt members of particular social groups physically or emotionally. Examples such as leaving raw bacon at a mosque and painting swastikas on the wall of a synagogue can all be characterized as bigotry.[7,8,9] By transferring the meaning of bigotry to the meaning of racism, members of the hegemonic culture allow themselves to be exonerated from wrongdoing, and therefore innocent of perpetrating social injustice.

Turning once more to Lopez, the concept of colorblindness will help us to understand the role that race (and by extension ethnicity, sexuality, etc.) plays in a broad social and political context. Instead of conceding that racism, as well as other forms of systematic discrimination, is not only at work in American society, but built directly into the economic, political, and cultural systems within it, the *colorblind* perspective uses a working model of an ideal world, in which one's skin color is neutralized. According to Lopez:

> Racism, in other words, has been reduced to broad generalizations about another group based on the color of their skin. It has become an individual construction as opposed to a social or civilizational construct. . . . The belief that colorblindness will eliminate racism is not only shortsighted but reinforces the notion that racism is a personal—as opposed to systemic—issue.[10]

PRACTICE: RACISM, HEGEMONY, BIGOTRY, AND COLORBLINDNESS

Ms. Q is from a predominantly white, upper-middle-class, suburban town, but always considered herself open-minded and unbiased. She has an affinity for movies starring black actors and books that handle racial issues. She believes that if she can show her students, most of whom are black, that they live in a negative neighborhood and have the power to get out, they can be successful, too. She designs much of her curriculum around this idea.

1. What are some of the messages that are conveyed in your daily life that perpetuate the idea of *racism*, as defined above?
2. In what ways are these messages sustained in schools in general? How about in your school in particular?
3. Can you pinpoint any elements of the cultural narrative to which you subscribe that may contribute to racism? Be honest, now; how do you contribute to racism as a result, either in your teaching or in your life?
4. Have you ever been a "victim" of bigotry or hatred? If so, please describe it. How can you use this experience to increase your empathy for others who also experience bigotry, perhaps on a more regular basis?
5. Can "colorblindness" be a reality in society? Why or why not? What about in schools or individual classrooms? If so, what is the difference?

BIAS

While the concepts of racism, bigotry, hegemony, and colorblindness serve an important role in understanding the process that leads to one's thought and behavior, bias is essential to explore when it comes to actual teaching practices. Bias, as is the case with many of the already mentioned concepts, can be elusive to define, revealing a number of different and seemingly valid ways to be conceptualized. One way to define bias is as a tendency, inclination, or prejudice toward or against something or someone.[11] In another, perhaps narrower sense, bias can be defined as an unfair personal opinion that influences one's judgment and/or actions.[12]

In either conception, the main working of bias is causing an individual, or group of individuals, to think or act in a particular way that either advances or regresses a particular process as a result of some preexisting conception of right and wrong. In this respect, it is very easy to understand how culture, and the corresponding cultural narrative, becomes an implicit factor in virtually every sort of bias, whether relatively innocuous, inadvertently oppressive, or blatantly discriminating.

Like racism, bias has become a weaponized concept, used primarily to disqualify the information, perspective, or influence of a particular person or organization. A current example is accusations of bias in the media, either in general or toward particular outlets.[13] In education, a relevant example is the difference in disciplinary practices between boys and girls, especially among children of racial and ethnic minorities.[14,15]

Cultural bias, then, is a particular type of bias that extends from one's cultural narrative. Because the concept of bias is weaponized, most people's initial reaction to regarding their own bias is to deny its existence. Much like racism, the connotation is that to admit that one is biased is to admit that one is hateful, and most do not like to consider themselves hateful. However, when the concept is disarmed, as it will be in this context, we realize that to admit our biases is simply to admit that we have different expectations of different people based on our narratives and experiences, and are likely to treat them differently as a result.

Specifically at work are what could be known as *cultural biases*, or modes of thinking and belief that place one's own culture as more relevant, and therefore practicable, than another's. Consider an experiment in which two groups of people, Westerners and non-Westerners (specifically from Liberia, Africa) were asked to sort objects. While Westerners tended to sort objects by linguistic category, such as food with other food and utensils with other utensils, the non-Westerners sorted the objects by function, such as pairing the knife with the potato, as the potato could be cut with a knife.[16]

Clearly, there is a difference in the modality of thinking employed by these two groups. However, if asked which was correct, most likely each group member would defend his or her methodology. Why might this be the case? It likely has to do with the cultural narrative and how the cultural narrative is adapted and used to apply meaning to activities of everyday life.

Westerners place a heavy emphasis on taxonomy and categorization, which is played out in a number of social actions, while other cultures do not, at least in the same manner. Additionally, as cultural narratives are essentially stories that are told and acted out regularly within the everyday workings of the culture, the language used to tell, reinforce, and employ the cultural narrative, as well as its meaning, is itself culturally determined.

The reflective question soon becomes, then, what are the cultural biases possessed by each individual and how do they influence what each individual does in the classroom? This is a difficult and complex question that requires much attention when attempting an answer, but one that is also quite worthy of introspection. To begin exploring your cultural biases, perhaps taking your thoughts about your own culture a bit deeper will help.

PRACTICE: NAMING YOUR CULTURE(S)

Ms. G considers herself a Puerto Rican, "born and bred." She intends to marry a Puerto Rican man and raise her children to be proud of their heritage, even if it means living in a neighborhood with challenges so they can be around "their kind." She doesn't believe that what she is doing is "self-segregation," and she believes she would welcome people of any culture into her family and house. However, she believes deeply in the Puerto Rican sense of the "family unit" and the importance that a shared heritage plays in its strength.

1. If you could give your culture a name, what would it be? If you need to choose two or three, you may do so.
2. For each of those names, come up with one or two "values" or "elements" of that culture that are essential. That is, if the culture "lost" that element, it would no longer be the same culture.
3. Think of one or two examples of how that element plays out in your life and/or your teaching.

The role of culture often has much more meaning when different cultures are attempting to create a new environment. For example, when individuals from a different country, with a different language, dressing style, and sense of social behavior, come to a country in which a dominant culture with a dominant language and dominant customs has already been established, a new environment is created. When both cultures begin interacting, there is likely to be conflict, and a process of attrition of certain cultural elements and retention and absorption of others is experienced on both sides.

For example, when a community experiences a large influx of Hispanic immigrants, there is likely to be more Spanish spoken in that community, Spanish restaurants opening, and Spanish-style groceries available, whether assented to by the original or preexisting community members or not. Therefore, more Spanish will be spoken in school, and teachers, administrators, and students alike will be forced to determine how this cultural change should be handled. Whether you are part of the existent group or the new group is likely to have a significant influence on how you view the potential changes.

While cultural bias is a significant factor in one's teaching, *confirmatory bias*, or the tendency to misinterpret new information as evidence for already-held beliefs and hypotheses, can be particularly pernicious in the classroom.[17] Indeed, these two concepts are not independent of one another, and one's cultural bias is likely at work in confirmatory bias, and vice versa. If an individual holds a deep enough belief in a concept or idea, he or she is likely to

PRACTICE: EXAMINING YOUR CULTURAL BEHAVIOR

Ms. J, a 29-year-old white teacher, has befriended Mr. Z, a new teacher in her district who is just a few years older than her. He is the only black teacher in the school, and just one of three in the district. On Friday a group of teachers, most of whom were also white and female, went out for after-work drinks at a local bar and grill. While there, a small group of likely intoxicated men began to make increasingly vocal comments about the "black dude" with the "white chicks." While Ms. J was concerned and upset, the other teachers responded by laughing along with them. Eventually Mr. Z said he had to go, and left the bar quickly.

1. Think of a time in which you were a member of what would be considered the "dominant" culture in a given situation. How did that "dominance" affect your comfort level, decision-making capabilities, or even power within your social group?
2. Now try to think of a time in which you were a member of what could be considered the "subculture." In what ways were your comfort level, decision-making capabilities, and power within the social group different?
3. What role did "control" play in both situations?

use newly obtained information to confirm the already-held idea, even when the new information is ambiguous or even contradictory to the belief.

For example, if a politician is unhappy with his or her poll numbers from particular sources, he or she may use such numbers to confirm that those reporting the results are inherently critical, and therefore cannot be trusted. In a similar sense, if a teacher and parent have a historically difficult relationship with one child, the teacher and parent may interpret one another's behavior for a second child in accordance with the already-held animosity.

But in what ways can bias directly affect the classroom climate? Perhaps the most relevant way is in the context of assessment. Assessment is central to teaching practice, and we as teachers engage in it regularly in formal as well as informal manners. What we often do not think about is how our assessment practices may not only reinforce but also be a direct outgrowth of our beliefs about our students, especially those who are from different cultures or communities than ourselves.

Assessments are synthesized measures, created by people, that can approximate, to one degree or another, how an individual responds to a stimulus. When assessments are standardized, that is, imply a "typical" range of responses to stimuli that reflect what one should be able to generate, it is asserted that there is a narrow space by which one can demonstrate his or her knowledge or skills. In this, however, lies an assumption, and a potentially dangerous one: that there is an expected way, perhaps even definitive, in which information should not only be known, but interpreted and expressed.

While standardized tests are often thought of as those commercially available assessments used for formal evaluations, diagnoses, and other educational measurements, standardized assessments are also those that will reflect what appears to be "standard," or expected within a curriculum or individual lesson. Therefore, whoever creates the assessment also asserts the standard by which it is to be measured and interpreted. This person, whether intentionally or not, invariably uses his or her own biases in the design, implementation, and evaluation of the assessment.

What is not considered is what variability may exist in the language, context, and format through which the assessment is implemented. These biases can be facilitated by multiple means, including meanings of words, effects of acculturation or assimilation, motivation, and communication style and response modality, among others.[18]

Wording is essential in an assessment, since the wording of a question is determinant of the type of response that is expected to be elicited. However, many teachers take meanings of words for granted, especially when those teachers share a cultural context. As an example, when members of certain Native American tribes are asked "what is the son of your aunt called?" most respond "brother," while "cousin" is the expected answer.

At face value, these respondents would likely not receive credit for this answer, and face a penalty on the assessment. This response is elicited, however, because in a number of Native American communities the term "brother" is used to refer to all boys of the same generation, not as a familial designation.[19] Can this answer, then, truly be considered incorrect when the very meaning of the word itself is different within a specific cultural context?

Acculturation, or the extent to which someone has adapted one's culture to another as a result of intercultural contact, can also present significant challenges to meaningful assessment. For example, students who come from cultures that have strong family ties, such as some Asian and Hispanic cultures, often show a significant difficulty acquiring English, as much time outside of school is spent with family who may only speak, or prefer to speak, their native language.

By extension, in schools in which English only is valued, students from non-English-speaking homes tend to show less-steady English acquisition, whereas students who attend schools in which multiple cultures are valued and native and English language is used make significant gains, as they are more content and comfortable. Similarly, if the students from other cultures or linguistic backgrounds are held to native English speakers, especially white students, as a comparison, they are more likely to be perpetually viewed as deficient.

One's sense of motivation is also connected to this idea, in that whether or not someone is driven by failure or success, or is provided positive or negative feedback, more often can be a strong determinant in how one performs on an assessment, especially when he or she is aware of being assessed. Additionally, the way in which an individual responds, and is therefore evaluated on his or her response, can also be an extension of culture.

Students from African American and certain Hispanic cultures may be much more accustomed to a "call-and-response" type of interaction, in which someone initiates a verbal interaction by calling out, and others respond chorally. This can be in direct contrast to the expected behavior of raising one's hand and waiting to be called on.

Therefore, children who come from a culture in which this type of interaction is acceptable are likely to be punished in a culture in which it is not,

PRACTICE: BIAS IN CLASSROOM ASSESSMENT

Mrs. M prefers to design her own curricular materials when she can. When teaching a science unit that involved fermentation, she shared a story in which a group of Catholic monks began to experiment with the fermentation process to learn how to make beer to support their monastery. In the short assessment section after the reading, she noticed that two of her students, cousins who were from Pakistan and both Muslim, did not answer three of the questions. When she reminded them to answer all the questions to ensure full credit, they told her they were not allowed to talk about alcohol because it was forbidden in their religion.

1. When you design an assessment, how much attention do you pay to the wording you use? Similarly, how much attention do you pay to the cultural and/or linguistic makeup of your class?
2. Is it important to hold students from different cultures or linguistic backgrounds to the same standard or level that native speakers are held to? Why or why not?
3. In what ways do your cultural expectations influence the classroom rules that you implement? Is it possible that the rules you implement do disadvantage certain types of students? Explain a bit.
4. In what ways might the students in your school who come from other cultural and/or linguistic backgrounds feel valued in your school as it directly relates to their culture? How might they feel excluded or devalued?

such as in a classroom when a teacher asks a question and expects a hand to be raised to signify readiness to answer. As another example, students who come from cultures in which prolonged eye contact can be interpreted as a challenge to authority may be confused by, and uncomfortable with, the requirement to maintain eye contact with the speaker in American schools.[20]

NOTES

1. Paulo Coelho. (1993). *The Alchemist*. New York: HarperOne.
2. Gerardo R. Lopez. (2003). "The (Racially Neutral) Politics of Education: A Critical Race Theory Perspective." *Educational Administration Quarterly*, *39*(1), 68–94.
3. Christopher J. Lyons & E. M. Pettit. (2011). "Compounded Disadvantage: Race, Incarceration, and Wage Growth." *Social Problems*, *58*(2), 257–280.
4. K. Paul-Emile. (2014). "Beyond Title VII: Rethinking Race, Ex-Offender Status, and Employment Discrimination in the Information Age." *Virginia Law Review*, *100*(5), 893–952.
5. Jordan Segall. (2011). "Mass Incarceration, Ex-Felon Discrimination, and Black Labor Market Disadvantage." *University of Pennsylvania Journal of Law and Social Change*, *14*, 159–182.
6. Nasruallah Mambrol. (2017). "Hegemony." *Literary Theory and Criticism*. Retrieved on September 6, 2019, from https://literariness.org/2017/10/10/hegemony.
7. Tara Sheets and J. D. Gallop. (2017). "Bacon Used in Hate Crime: Titusville Man Gets 15 Years in Mosque Vandalism." *Florida Today*. Retrieved on September 6, 2019, from https://www.floridatoday.com/story/news/crime/2017/12/05/titusville-man-sentenced-15-years-prison-after-mosque-vandalism/924987001/.
8. William K. Rashbaum and Ali Winston. (2018). "Ilana Glazer Event Canceled After Anti-Semitic Graffiti Is Found." *New York Times*. Retrieved September 6, 2019, from https://www.nytimes.com/2018/11/02/nyregion/broad-city-jewish-synagogue-anti-semitism.html.
9. Associated Press. (2016). "Decorated Officer Charged With Threatening Muslims in North Carolina." Retrieved September 6, 2019, from https://www.nytimes.com/2016/06/12/us/decorated-officer-charged-with-threatening-muslims-in-north-carolina.html.
10. Lopez, 2003, p. 69.
11. https://www.psychologytoday.com/us/basics/bias.
12. https://dictionary.cambridge.org/us/dictionary/english/bias.
13. Ceren Budak, S. Goel, & J. Rao. (2016). "Fair and Balanced: Quantifying Media Bias through Crowdsourced Content Analysis." *Public Opinion Quarterly*, *80*(S1), 250–271.
14. Anne Gregory, R. Skiba, & P. A. Noguera. (2011). "The Achievement Gap and the Discipline Gap: Two Sides of the Same Coin?" *Educational Researcher*, *39*(1), 59–68.

15. Duane E. Thomas & H. Stevenson. (2009). "Gender Risks and Education: The Particular Classroom Challenges of Low-Income African-American Boys." *Review of Research in Education*, *33*(1), 160–180.

16. Michael Cole, J. Gay, J. Glick, & D. W. Sharp. (1971). *The Cultural Context of Learning and Thinking*. New York: Basic Books.

17. Lea-Rachel D. Kosnik. (2008). "Refusing to Budge: A Confirmatory Bias in Decision Making." *Mind & Society*, *7*(2), 193–214.

18. Kyung Hee Kim & D. Zabelina. (2015). "Cultural Bias in Assessment: Can Creativity Assessment Help?" *International Journal of Critical Pedagogy*, *6*(2), 129–148.

19. C. M. Shields. (1997). "Learning About Assessment from Native American Schools: Advocacy and Empowerment." *Theory Into Practice*, *36*, 102–109.

20. Kim & Zabelina, 2015.

Part II

PRACTICING AS A REFLECTIVE TEACHER

Chapter Six

Us and Them

Cultural Responsiveness and the Reflective Teacher

> "Many of us walk around with too many answers. The right question, of course, can often be the key that unlocks the universe."[1]
>
> —Lama Surya Das

As the adage goes, change is the only constant. This holds particularly true for the demographics of American public schools. While there are most certainly varied responses to this trend, what remains inarguable is that students from diverse backgrounds will be finding themselves among one another in America's classrooms at an increasing level, and teachers must be well prepared to respond to each of these students in a positive, constructive, and productive manner.

Indeed, this shift can be an opportunity for American children and teachers to embrace new cultures and use their differences to expand and deepen American culture. This ideal, however, is not as often the reality. Naming the problem directly, scholar Monica Brown suggests:

> The dramatic demographic shift in the United States is more apparent in the public schools than anywhere else. But this change in the racial, cultural, and linguistic diversity of the student population is not the problem. The problem lies in the way educators have responded to that change. . . . As a result, educators are trying to develop a closer fit between students' home cultures, and the culture of the school.[2]

The reality of the conversation, however, is much more complex and much more socially risky, especially in a culture that can be quite fragile when it comes to issues of racial and ethnic diversity, and its relation to systematic power structures. Geneva Gay, a leader in socioeducational studies, confronts the issue in clear though humbling terms, especially as it stands for white teachers:

> While most teachers are not blatant racists, many probably are cultural hegemonists. They expect all students to behave according to the school's cultural standards of normality. When students of color fail to comply, the teachers find them unlovable, problematic, and difficult to honor or embrace without equivocation.[3]

The answer, therefore, is quite clear, but regrettable for many of us. That is, what is regarded as "normal" in most classrooms is reflective primarily, if not only, of white Eurocentric conceptions of behavior and etiquette. With roughly 80 percent of teachers being white females[4] and most school-level administrators also white but relatively even by gender,[5] these cultural assumptions remain fixed and largely unchallenged.

Situating a culturally diversifying student body within a largely stagnant and dominant cultural faculty and administration will create, then, a deeply disproportionate cultural system indisputably governed by white Eurocentric values, traditions, definitions of knowledge and success, curricular materials, and social rules. Even in schools with a dominant nonwhite student body, the

PRACTICE: CULTURAL HEGEMONY IN SCHOOLS

Mr. J just got a job teaching in a seventh-grade English language arts class in a predominantly black and Hispanic suburban school. Knowing that the students in this school had a reputation for being "disrespectful to authority," Mr. J thought that if he devised a clear set of rules and a behavior contract the students would sign, he would be able to establish a sense of authority with the students. The behavior contract included rules such as "no talking until you are called on" and "raise your hand when you have a comment."

1. If you are white, in what ways have you upheld a "hegemonic" cultural understanding in your classrooms? If you are not white, what have been your experiences with white teachers either as a student or colleague?
2. If you teach in a diverse district, is it reasonable to expect all students to behave in the same way regardless of culture? If you live in a district that is predominantly one race, culture, ethnicity or another, should the "dominant" student culture be most reflected?
3. If you teach in a homogeneous district, should the students receive curricular materials that reflect their culture or heritage only, or others as well? Is it different for a predominantly white district?

staff is most likely white, resulting in the same cultural assumptions but even deeper cultural disconnect.

How, then, can this cultural imbalance be addressed? The curricular paradigm that addresses this question has come to be known as culturally responsive pedagogy (or sometimes culturally responsive teaching), which has been conceptualized in a number of ways. According to Dave Brown:

> Culturally responsive teaching involves purposely responding to the needs of the many culturally and ethnically diverse learners in classrooms. It involves specifically student-oriented instructional processes as well as choosing and delivering ethnically and culturally relevant curricula . . . [and] uses communication processes that reflect students' values and beliefs held about learning, the responsibilities of teachers, and the roles of students in school settings.[6]

According to Geneva Gay:

> Culturally responsive teaching is defined as using the cultural characteristics, experiences, and perspectives of ethnically diverse students as conduits for teaching them more effectively. It is based on the assumption that when academic knowledge and skills are situated within the lived experiences and frames of references of students, they are more personally meaningful, have a higher interest appeal, and are learned more easily and thoroughly.

Through both of these definitions, the relevance of academic curricula is directly related to the meaning and accessibility of the concepts being taught to the students. One example comes from one of my own students, in which she was relating a story about playing in her backyard to a class of predominantly black students in an urban school. When she realized that her students did not appear to be responding to the story, she explored it with them and realized that many did not know what a backyard was (they all lived in urban complexes), and the ones that did had never actually been in one.

Changing her analogy to a park with a basketball court, which many had just outside their homes, allowed the content to become more relevant and therefore meaningful. This teacher demonstrated her cultural bias by assuming that the concept of a backyard was universal but employed cultural responsiveness when she realized that it was not, and as a result adjusted the frame of reference to one that was relevant to her students.[7]

Understanding the connection that culturally responsive pedagogy has to critical pedagogy becomes particularly important, then, when we begin to relate it to actual teaching practices. As Michael Vavrus puts it:

> [culturally responsive pedagogy] developed out of tensions within a society that aspires to unified democratic ideals and goals while being demographically composed of a culturally and linguistically diverse multicultural population.[8]

Essentially, critical pedagogy situates the purpose of schooling squarely within obtaining a truly democratic and socially just society, yielding teaching as not just a manner of sharing or transmitting information, but as a deeply political act responsible for exposing and replacing elements of hegemony with expanded power of marginalized groups.

BECOMING A CULTURALLY RESPONSIVE TEACHER

While the concept of culturally responsive pedagogy was introduced, it is further important to explore what it means to become a culturally responsive teacher. This requires deep reflection and honest introspection involving one's own biases and expectations, and what assumptions one makes about his or her classroom environment. Since these notions are direct outgrowths of one's culture and its corresponding narrative, one must earnestly begin to question the depth and breadth of how those messages play out in actual instructional practices. This introspection leads to the first element of becoming a culturally responsive teacher, which is developing a culturally diverse knowledge base.[9]

While many teachers are likely to suggest that the vast majority of teacher training happens "on the job," there is little question that the discussions and exposures one has to the content and theories of teaching in a higher-education setting are an integral part of one's teacher identity, whether it is regarded as such or not. An exploration of the demographics of the professoriate is an appropriate start. In 2018, the US Department of Education reported that of the 1.5 million professors employed in the United States, nearly 75 percent of the professoriate was white, while black and Hispanic professors collectively represented only 5 percent, and Asian professors 6 percent.[10]

While it is possible that of these predominantly white professors, many may be critically minded and racially and ethnically conscious, this does not mean that the lived experiences of nonwhite cultures could be conveyed by them. With only 10 percent of the professoriate consisting of nonwhites, it becomes nearly impossible for college and university students to receive a firsthand account of racial experiences different from those of white professors, forcing them to rely on their own experiences or interpretations of outsiders' ideas.

Teachers must become familiar with particular cultural practices and beliefs such as interpretations of communality and the role of the family, modes of social interaction, especially between children and adults, and implications of gender roles. For example, while many teachers lament the lack of time that Hispanic children spend on homework as opposed to attending soccer (fútbol) games, the central role that these games play in the social and political functionality of these communities themselves is quite often overlooked.[11,12]

Gathering factual information from authentic sources, such as people directly from various communities' institutions (civic groups, religious institutions, libraries, business owners) can deepen one's understanding of the culture significantly, especially when that information deepens one's understanding of the social and cultural significance of the issue.[13]

The tendency for teachers to regard practices of different cultures that "distract" students from the importance of school grows directly out of a cultural deficiency model; that is, elements of other cultures that appear to work against values of the dominant culture are a form of "weakness," which needs to be remediated and replaced. Choosing to attend or play soccer games, having a job to contribute to the family means, or taking care of younger siblings, while ranging in leisurely to obligatory, all act as means of reinforcing the cultural deficiency model. Statements from this perspective take the form of "If they would only spend as much time on schoolwork as they did on ________, they would be so much better off."

While intended to be helpful, this frame of mind is completely based in a hegemonic cultural perspective. Contrasting this scornful interpretation of current immigrant families with the ways that white European descendants often laud their own ancestors' sacrifices can be particularly revealing about how the immigrant story can change with the later achievement of cultural dominance.

Out of the cultural deficiency model grows a mode of education that is based in facilitating assimilation. Assimilation, we imagine, is the best way for children of different backgrounds to become contributing members of American society. Elements such as learning English (or its extreme cousin "English-only education"), dressing in American-style clothing, associating with white people, all contribute to the idea that much, if not most, of one's "native" culture must be sacrificed in order to achieve true success in a Western (or American) context. Schools, then, become the grounds for which such assimilation is not only fostered, but taught and valued.

Instead of a cultural deficiency model, which necessitates an assimilating process, culturally responsive teachers must employ and maintain a cultural difference model. That is, identifying cultural differences not for the sake of replacing them, but for the sake of incorporating them, if not using them, to maintain and learn to value the most important elements of their students' cultures.

PRACTICE: BEGINNING TO CULTIVATE CULTURAL RESPONSIVENESS

Ms. K works in a district that has a high population of El Salvadoran and Colombian immigrants. While her students are polite and well-behaved, she has a problem with them completing their homework. When she explores why, many of her students tell her that they go to soccer games often until 8 or 9 o'clock, and have to put their younger siblings to bed while their parents go back to work. Wanting to learn more, she decides to attend a game herself and sees that her students' families are all there, interacting in loving and celebratory ways. She also finds out that the parents, as much as they can, will save their lunch/dinner breaks for this time, as it is the only chance they get to see their children for most of the week.

1. Think of a "stereotype" that is often maintained in your school about another culture's "approach" toward school. Explore whether you are likely to regard this difference as a deficiency. If so, try to come up with another way of interpreting it that is based in cultural difference instead.
2. How have you tried to address the cultural differences in your class in a positive way? Think of some examples. Now, evaluate whether this activity maintained exploration at the "surface level," or whether it went deeper. Either way, expand on what you can do in the future to take it even deeper.
3. Identify something you don't understand about another culture that you've found "interferes" with school. Now, try to come up with a possible explanation from a positive perspective (that is, how this practice or tendency might be a positive trait, rather than a negative one).

This requires a conscious shift from a hegemonic perspective to a power-sharing perspective, and one in which the teachers may even need to sacrifice some of their authority to their students. These are teachers who can admit and confront their ignorance and allow their students, and their students' families, to educate and replace some of their long-held cultural beliefs.

FACILITATING A CULTURALLY RESPONSIVE CLASSROOM

Creating a culturally responsive environment is a wholly expansive process. Rather than working from a perspective that seeks to narrow curriculum into clearly defined components of content, culturally responsive teachers seek to broaden their instructional and material resources so as to continually provide room for multiple perspectives.

This process requires a number of components that are different from, if not opposite to, traditional classrooms, including an initial focus on building relationships with students through dialogue and exploration, establishing the classroom space and curriculum as a forum for culturally relevant resources provided in a safe and nonjudgmental manner, and providing curriculum content in culturally relevant and culturally reflective ways, even if they are different from one's own deep-seated cultural expectations.

In order to establish valuable and respectful understandings of students' cultures in a classroom with cultural diversity, the teacher must be willing to display his or her ignorance in the spirit of learning. That is, many teachers approach the beginning of a school year as a means of establishing their authority or leadership (the aphorism "don't smile until Christmas" captures this particular spirit of teaching). Even teachers who approach this process in an inclusive or mild manner are still maintaining a power-based dynamic in which the students are established as the "listeners" while the teacher is established as the "speaker."

However, a culturally responsive teacher who does not share a culture with her students must take an opposite stance. Because it is immediately apparent to her students that she is not "one of them," this mismatch must be named and addressed quickly, compassionately, and in the spirit of learning. While teachers are often given the message that they should remain "neutral" in a classroom environment, such neutrality is not only inutile, it is entirely impossible, even in a situation when the class is made up of predominantly white students, as what is regarded as "neutrality" is really hegemony.

The teacher can begin to engage in a cultural exploration by beginning the class with an "introduce yourself" activity that relates directly to culture. In this activity the teacher can begin by introducing herself, naming his or her culture, and relating that he or she is "excited to learn about all of your different cultures." Then the children can go around the room and do the same, being allowed to name their culture however they would like.

Each culture can then be individually acknowledged and validated (perhaps even recorded and displayed). The teacher can then explore what the students' families are like, such as what languages are spoken, what holidays or special occasions are celebrated, what are the important values held by each family, and the like. These conversations can lead to multiple culturally based activities, all of which establish the classroom's cultural diversity as the valued norm.[14]

Once this cultural comfort and knowledge is established, the teacher can begin to incorporate elements of each culture into the academic environment.

Simple adjustments such as using culturally relevant names in word problems and teacher-created stories can begin to establish the cultural relevance of the academic curriculum.

However, this is not enough. The teacher must establish the cultural relevance of all of the materials in the classroom by choosing books that not only reflect the faces and bodies of the students in the classroom, but also handle culturally relevant activities and referents for the children, establish and explore the stories and struggles of cultural leaders, and permit questions that may be critical or indicative of cultural frustrations.

Finally, a perceived paradox must also be addressed as cultural responsiveness applies to classrooms that are made up of predominantly white students. While cultural responsiveness hinges on reproducing and reflecting likeness in classrooms for students of color, the opposite is true in classrooms for students that are predominantly white.

This reversal is based on the very notion of hegemony and, when understood, becomes clear in its necessity. That is, from the critical pedagogical and culturally responsive perspective, normality, as it applies to most school academic and behavioral cultures, is modeled after the white Eurocentric code of values. As such, everything that follows it is naturally in line with this code, except where it is intentionally disrupted.

Therefore, predominantly white classrooms are environments in which this code must be disrupted in order to foster awareness of different cultures'

PRACTICE: BUILDING A CULTURALLY RESPONSIVE CLASSROOM

In celebration of Black History Month, Mr. K decides he is going to read a book about Jesse Owens. One of his students asks why they only read books about black people in February.

1. Think of the curriculum materials you use in your classroom (books, examples, videos) and discuss whether they are truly culturally responsive or not. What can you do to enhance the cultural responsiveness of these materials?
2. Engaging in cultural conversations requires naming and discussing elements that are often regarded as "off-limits" in public schools. How might this be handled in your district? What are your concerns about having such conversations?
3. The difference between how cultural responsiveness in a diverse classroom as opposed to a predominantly white classroom should be handled was offered. What are your thoughts about this?

realities. Since the white Eurocentric world and its corresponding social codes are continuously reflected back to white students, culturally responsive classrooms, in this case, must ensure that the experiences of nonwhite students are also present and, whenever possible, expressed and facilitated by an individual who is a part of that particular culture. Additionally, as culture goes beyond race and ethnicity, finding existing cultural differences within these classrooms is also a valuable tool to enhance cultural competence in an otherwise homogeneous environment.

NOTES

1. Lama Surya Das. (2007). *Awakening the Buddhist Heart: Integrating Love, Meaning, and Connection into Every Part of Your Life*. New York: Potter/Ten Speed/Harmony/Rosedale.
2. Monica R. Brown. (2007). "Educating All Students: Creating Culturally Responsive Teachers, Classrooms, and Schools." *Intervention in School & Clinic*, *43*(1), 57–62.
3. Geneva Gay. (2000). *Culturally Responsive Teaching: Theory, Research, and Practice*. New York: Teachers College Press.
4. US Department of Education. (2019). National Center for Education Statistics. (NCES-2018-070).
5. US Department of Education. (2018). National Center for Education Statistics.
6. Dave F. Brown. (2004). "Management Strategies: Reflection of Culturally Responsive Teaching." *Urban Education*, *39*(3), 266–289.
7. Sabrina Cuccia. (2019). Personal communication, St. Joseph's College. Story used with permission.
8. M. Vavrus. (2008). "Culturally Responsive Teaching." In M. Good (Ed.), *21st Century Teaching: A Reference Handbook*. Thousand Oaks, CA: Sage.
9. Gay, 2000.
10. US Department of Education, National Center for Education Statistics. (2018). *The Condition of Education*. (NCES 2018-144).
11. Andrew M. Lindner & D. N. Hawkins. (2012). "Globalization, Culture Wars, and Attitudes Toward Soccer in America: An Empirical Assessment of How Soccer Explains the World." *The Sociological Quarterly*, *53*(1), 68–91.
12. Carlos R. Stoneham. (2015). "The Role of Soccer in Latin American Culture. Soccer Politics: A Discussion Forum About the Power of the Global Game." Retrieved on September 14, 2019, from https://sites.duke.edu/wcwp/2015/02/06/the-role-of-soccer-in-latin-american-culture/.
13. Geneva Gay. (2002). "Preparing for Culturally Responsive Teaching." *Journal of Teacher Education*, *53*(2), 106–116.
14. Heraldo V. Richards, A. Brown, & T. Forde. (2007). "Addressing Diversity in Schools: Culturally Responsive Pedagogy." *Teaching Exceptional Children*, *39*(3), 64–68.

Chapter Seven

Making Peace with Ourselves

Peace Education and the Reflective Teacher

> "Just as you love to consider what to do to help yourself, so should you love to consider what to do to help others."[1]
>
> —Nagarjuna

Culturally responsive teaching was offered as a means of embracing and exploring the differences between cultures represented in one's classroom, and offered a means to create a fully inclusive, safe, and constructive environment in which members of the classroom community can simultaneously expand their understandings and give root to their own identities. This type of pedagogy will allow students to become familiar and comfortable with differing views, beliefs, and opinions in a way that is productive and incorporative rather than regressive.

However, more is needed if these lessons are to take hold and influence greater society once these students move on from the safer and more controlled school environment. As Dewey reminds us, what is learned in school directly affects society in terms of continuity, or the lasting influence of the learning experience, and interaction, or how that learning experience will directly affect one's future social actions.[2]

Peace education, therefore, will be explored as the next step in how a reflective teacher can create a cabal of reflective students. According to Kevin Kester:

> [Peace education is] a mechanism for the transformation from a culture of violence to a culture of peace through a process of "conscientization." By raising consciousness of people to their world, their rights, and the issues at the core of our contemporary terrene—through exploration of our common values and aspirations—it is possible to negotiate a shared future based on love, respect, and human dignity.[3]

Ian Harris explains it this way:

> Peace education informs about the dangers of violence and ways to achieve peace. Peace educators provide information about peace strategies that address many different forms of violence. Because there are so many different forms of violence, both international and domestic, peace education varies within differing cultures and contexts [such as] personal, interpersonal, international, domestic, intercultural, civil, and environmental peace.[4]

While many would dismiss such a perspective as idealistic and suited more for a theory than a pedagogy, there is a strong body of research to suggest that such movement, though difficult, is possible, but requires a marked paradigmatic shift from traditional educational values and practices. Indeed, in a commercialistic and positivistic culture that insists on quick and "measurable" results in return for investments, peace education, in its incremental and largely social context, is often unseen as a priority form of curriculum worth investing in.

Teachers, however, who are on the front lines of the educational process can play an integral role in the advocacy for peace education in schools. The first step in building a classroom able to engage in a peace education curriculum involves reflection on how the current system engages in and perpetuates a curriculum of violence.

In order to understand this, the definition of violence must be broadened and recontextualized from a focus of *physical* violence to also include *intellectual* violence. One way in which intellectual violence is practiced in schools is the perpetuation of the notion that teachers and administrators uniquely know the truth and that, essentially, ultimate deference must be paid to them by the students. This practice reinforces student passivity and complacence and strips away any power held by the students. Those students who are eventually empowered, at least in part, often earn that as a privilege when they are deemed safe enough to do so, such as in gifted and talented or enrichment programs.

A second way in which traditional schools enact intellectual violence is through the compulsory practice and reinforcement of competition, which, even when collaborative efforts are also fostered, often overshadows them with outside cultural reinforcement. This focus on competition creates an adversarial environment in which resources are regarded as being dispersed only to the deserving. Finally, policies that use force, either physical or intellectual, to control students often lead to an overuse of such power, almost inevitably relegating certain students to the receiving end of harsh discipline.

PRACTICE: NAMING VIOLENCE IN THE SCHOOL CURRICULUM

Kevin is a bright and inquisitive child, thought likely to be gifted by a number of his teachers. However, Kevin is often unstimulated by the structure of the curriculum in his classroom and, as a result, physically acts out in frustration. Because Kevin is large for his age and his teacher is a smaller female, she often resorts to calling security to handle Kevin's outbursts, who bring him to a "calm-down" room, which is a basement closet, often for over an hour.

1. Do you believe peace education is an idealistic myth or a possibility? Explain a bit.
2. In what ways may have the regulations you set up in your classroom, either curricular or disciplinary, instilled a sense of intellectual violence? Try to give some examples.
3. How might you begin to rectify some of those instances of classroom violence?

FRAMING PEACE EDUCATION

Without a framework, the shape of what peace education can look like in a classroom remains elusive and risks becoming but another unrealized educational theory among many. However, with a viable framework, teachers can begin to see that peace education is a practice of substance, not just ideals, and can truly lead to change. It requires patience and appreciation of small markers of development and progress, but progress, nonetheless. As Tony Jenkins describes it, the ultimate purpose of peace education is to "educate for the formation of values consistent with peace and the norms that uphold it."[5]

Noted education activists and instructional pioneers David and Roger Johnson offer a viable framework for practicing peace education in contemporary schools.[6] First, they note the necessity for a "compulsory" attendance policy that is both enforceable and fair.

While many would suggest that American schools already have such a policy, it is important to note that such policies are largely unenforced, especially in socioeconomically challenged and predominantly racial minority areas, and that attendance does, indeed, have a substantial effect on school success.[7] Therefore, teachers must take heed of this trend and determine ways in which attendance can be valued by the student and his or her family.

Second, schools must become increasingly integrated and safe, providing spaces in which disputing groups can not only coexist peacefully, but engage in cooperative problem-solving processes through fostering conversation and cross-cultural understanding. In this context, all students must be granted and maintain equal status, regardless of their past.

Through deliberate and systematic integration, students may begin to develop positive interdependence, through which they may form new, mutual cultural identities while being able to maintain existing ones. Such interdependence can be obtained by establishing shared governance practices with equal representation among groups (involvement in student government, student activity committees); allowing for maintenance of essential cultural practices (wearing religious or cultural garments, using home languages in certain contexts); and allowing for collaborative determination of curricular materials, content, and activities.

Finally, allowing students, as a collective, to identify, handle, and resolve potential or actual conflicts is essential. Practices such as student-designed governance structures (including representation and checks and balances), due process, arrangements to increase "buy-in" to such processes, and developing skills to constructively handle disputes of any nature, all allow students to increase their civic awareness and responsibilities and develop the skills to carry such abilities to their lives postschool.

The cultural context of peace education, then, becomes essential in the actual practice of peace education. That is, with the established importance of the cultural narrative and its direct effect on teachers' and students' behavior, in order to engage in peace education practices, teachers must incorporate such elements into their guiding cultural narrative to create, essentially, an overarching culture of peace.[8]

By extension, the culture of peace must also incorporate the unconditional practice of healing and understanding. Indicative in this process is the importance of all parties, especially those conflicting, to be able to feel safe in expressing understandings and interpretation of conflict without the risk of judgment, scorn, or retaliation.

A good example of this idea can be found in a study by Israeli researchers Yigal Rosen and Gavriel Salomon, who in their work with Israeli and Palestinian youth demonstrated that while peace education practices may not necessarily affect the core beliefs of individuals' cultural understandings of conflict, they can influence their peripheral understandings. These peripheral changes, while small, may be sufficient to create enough space for continuing productive conversation, which was also shown to be essential to the peace education process.[9]

PRACTICE: SOWING THE SEEDS OF PEACE EDUCATION

Jimena is a young lady from an Ecuadoran immigrant family. While most of her family lives in a different part of the city, Jimena lives in a neighborhood that is mostly black, since it is close to where her mother and father work. One evening on her way home from dinner with her family, her father accidentally bumped into a young black man, who became enraged and pushed Jimena's father to the ground. Getting up quickly, the father, along with the rest of the family, ran back to their apartment. Now they only leave when they have to. The class, however, is made up of primarily black children.

1. In what ways has conflict occurred in your classroom among your students? Has there ever been a cultural nature to that conflict? If so, how did that make the resolution process different?
2. Do you, as a teacher, feel qualified to engage in conflict resolution? Was it a part of your teacher education program? Was it a part of teacher training or professional development at your school?
3. What have you done in your classroom to involve or empower your students to handle their own conflicts? Have they been successful?

PRACTICING PEACE EDUCATION IN THE CLASSROOM

As the philosophy of peace education is highly nontraditional and requires a shift in paradigm, so does its practice. Therefore, if any headway is to be truly made in the application of peace education practices, teachers and administrators must gain comfort in activities, instructional methodologies, and approaches that are likely to be considered unorthodox, or at the very least nontraditional. As Kevin Kester puts it:

> Educational practice must be consistent with the message of the education itself. If the goal is to create an engaged, critical, and active citizenry, valuing knowledge, understanding, skills, identity, and peaceful coexistence, then the philosophy and pedagogy used in the educational process must reflect this. The practice of authoritarian teaching, hence, is inconsistent with the transformative objective of peace education.[10]

Perhaps the first frame that a teacher can use to begin to introduce peace education practices in the classroom is through "constructive controversy." Because civil discourse is of paramount importance in the development of peace, learning to disagree constructively is an essential element of the practice. Teachers, then, can use a common (and somewhat innocuous) problem to begin to introduce the idea of constructive controversy. For example, a teacher might propose a change in the school lunch policy that would implement a discontinuation of serving chocolate milk and juice as an option, and only provide plain, low-fat milk and water.

Once reactions are gauged and the students have a short but sufficient time to air their initial grievances, the teacher can organize a system of deliberate discourse, or situations in which the students can discuss various advantages and disadvantages of such an action. Groups of children can then be charged with researching different merits and weaknesses of this policy, as well as developing some type of alternative policy they may propose. Once the students become comfortable with methodologies of researching problems before making judgments about them, the issues presented can become increasingly controversial.[11]

Second, teachers may wish to begin to instill the idea of negotiation and peer mediation. As a cornerstone of peace education is the transferral of power, especially justice-based power, to the student body, empowering students to enact their own systems of justice can be useful. While serious offenses such as physical violence and property destruction should not be left to the students, social infractions can, indeed, be relegated to student resolution almost entirely.

In almost all cases, teachers implement a social code in their classrooms, many of which likely have commonalities (e.g., respectful listening, one person talks at a time, no intimidation, etc.). These rules, though reasonable, are essentially imposed on the students without much, if any, constructive discussion. However, providing the students direct engagement in the formulation of the rules (even if they are not, in the end, different) as well as examples of infractions and related consequences can send a strong message of ownership in the classroom community.

Such a process is a powerful exercise in Deweyan democracy. For Dewey, democracy is an essential component of any socially just community, including classrooms. According to Dewey:

> Democracy is not simply defined as shared common interest, but reliance upon the social recognition and implications of mutual interests with its moral and ideal being the opportunity for all to develop their distinctive capacities . . . [it is] a means of associated living made up of individuals who participate in an interest so that each one has to refer one's own action to that of others, and consider the action of others to give point and direction to one's own.[12]

In this sense, the community itself does not reinforce extreme individualism and is inherently dependent on social referencing between all parties. This type of social contract can be the framework for the justice system designed in the classroom. Therefore, in a Deweyan democracy, the goal of conflict resolution is not to win; neither is it to simply find the "best common denominator" through compromise. Rather, it is to use the social system itself to determine how best the shared goals and interests of the classroom can be realized and do so in a collective and collaborative way.

Third, and quite similarly to culturally responsive pedagogy, all students in the class must be given an equal opportunity to share their cultural belief systems, traditions, rituals, and values with everyone else in a nonjudgmental manner. While activities involving "multicultural" learning have become commonplace in education, many if not most of these activities remain superficial.

That is, multicultural fairs sharing international food, clothing, and music are passed off as genuine experiences in multicultural learning and experience. While these elements are important, it is essential to deepen such experiences and explore the historical, social, and political context that led to such narratives and practices and examine how and why they may have changed.

For example, while the notion of "watermelon" is often used as a stereotypical, and often pejorative, image for blacks in America, few are aware of the deep historical and positive roots of the connection between freed blacks and watermelon, which they grew and sold independently, becoming a powerful symbol of their newfound freedom in the latter part of the 19th century. Exploring this narrative can be an effective and poignant means of how images can be colonized and rebranded for any number of social and political purposes.[13]

PRACTICE: PRACTICING PEACE THROUGH CLASSROOM INSTRUCTION

1. Try to deepen your understanding of each of these practices through some additional research. Then try to come up with some simple ways that you can employ them in your classroom.
2. Set some "peace education" goals either for yourself or with colleagues as a collaborative. Then design some "fully functional" lesson plans that can be of service to these goals.

NOTES

1. Robert A. F. Thurman. (1986). "Guidelines for Buddhist Social Activism Based on Nagarjuna's 'Jewel Garland of Royal Counsels.'" *The Tibet Journal, 11*(4), 8–34.

2. Eric Shyman. (2011). "A Comparison of Concepts of Democracy and Experience in a Sample of Major Works by Dewey and Freire." *Educational Philosophy and Theory*, *43*(10), 1035–1046.

3. Kevin Kester. (2008). "Peace Education: Experience and Storytelling as Living Education." *Peace & Conflict Review, 2*(2), 1–14.

4. Ian Harris. (2002). "Challenges for Peace Educators at the Beginning of the 21st Century." *Social Alternatives*, *21*(1), 28–31.

5. Tony Jenkins. (2004). "Comprehensive Programme and Course Planning Frameworks for the University of Peace Master's Degree Programme in Peace Education." Teachers College, Columbia University.

6. David W. Johnson & R. T. Johnson. (2005). "Essential Components of Peace Education." *Theory into Practice*, *44*(4), 280–292.

7. Douglas D. Ready. (2010). "Socioeconomic Disadvantage, School Attendance, and Early Cognitive Development: The Differential Effects of School Exposure." *Sociology of Education*, *83*(4), 271–286.

8. H. B. Danesh. (2006). "Towards an Integrative Theory of Peace Education." *Journal of Peace Education*, *3*(1), 55–78.

9. Yigal Rosen & G. Salomon. (2011). "Durability of Peace Education in the Shadow of Conflict." *Social Psychology of Education, 14*, 135–147.

10. Kester, 2008, p. 4.

11. David W. Johnson & R. T. Johnson. (2010). "Peace Education in the Classroom: Creating Effective Peace Education Programs." In G. Salomon & E. Cairns (Eds.), *Handbook on Peace Education* (pp. 223–240). New York: Psychology Press.

12. Shyman, 2011.

13. William Black. (2014, December). "How Watermelons Became a Racist Trope." *The Atlantic*.

Chapter Eight

Thinking and Acting

The Teacher as Scholar-Activist

"To know even one life has breathed easier because you have lived. This is the meaning of success."[1]

—Ralph Waldo Emerson

Teachers are scholars, whether they are aware of it or not; and teachers are activists, whether they are aware of it or not. The very act of teaching is political, and political movements, particularly the successful ones, are perpetuated, to one degree or another, by both scholars and activists. Indeed, as noted critical educator Michael Apple reminds us, "I and many others have argued that teaching must be seen as a political act."[2]

Anything political, if it is to be just and lasting without the necessity of force or coercion, must be based on the incessant seeking of the truth. This is the true purpose of scholarship. Teachers, therefore, are the most important scholars, as they are on the front lines, unprotected as they are, testing the theories, ideas, and postulates presented without the more sheltered walls of the college or university; determining whether these ideas can truly penetrate learning, or whether they are merely the meanderings of thinkers. By accepting this important position, teachers become obligated, perhaps unwittingly, to be well versed in the theory and discourse in their field, especially as it relates to both policy and practice, and become the truth bearers.

Perhaps the biggest challenge facing most teachers, beginning or otherwise, is the notion of "apprenticeship of observation." This term, credited to Dan Lortie in an influential paper from 1975, describes the phenomenon whereby student teachers, and practicing teachers by extension, begin their training process having already experienced several thousand hours of observation as a student. There are few if any other fields with such an informal yet persistent introduction.[3] For example, medical trainees have likely been to the doctor, but are not likely to gauge their entire perception of being a doctor based on those experiences, and are likely more willing to be aware of holes in their expertise.

Student teachers, however, appear to be quite different, and there is a certain level of assumption made based wholly on their experience. That is, teacher trainees mistake their classroom experience as students for the whole of the educators' experience, not realizing that the classroom teaching element is only a part of educators' experience.[4]

How, then, can teacher educators and cooperating teachers begin to unwork and replace the misconceptions and misperceptions of student teachers, some of whom already have a false sense of their own expertise and experience level? This becomes the problem of scientists or scholars who must harness their own understanding of the teacher training process as well as their own more legitimate expertise in order to reteach and rework these misconceptions.

TEACHERS AS SOCIAL SCIENTISTS

The purpose of social science, and social scientists, is to challenge and upset the deep-seated assumptions within participants of a society in order to expose and change them. In education, these deep-seated assumptions can take the form of biased curricula, assumptions about behavioral appropriateness, expected and accepted communication styles, and modalities of instruction. However, social science, over the course of its development, has in many cases abandoned its socially significant purpose, and instead became an insular exercise in writing and expounding primarily, if not exclusively, for other academics and scholars with little, if any, connection to actual social change. As Frey and Carragee suggest:

> Over the years . . . higher educational institutions tended to abandon [their] civic mission in favor of research toward a relatively small . . . group of fellow scholars . . . [as a result of] the privileging of "theory" over "application" in the academy . . . scholars are supposed to be spectators whose work is best done by looking at and contemplating what occurs without trying to affect it.[5]

The privilege of the academic social scientist is clear in this case, as there is ever the availability of the academy to hide within. Practicing teachers, however, have no hiding places and, as such, are the real social scientists; those who must know both theory and how to apply it, as well as handle the consequences of its failings and others' misgivings and critique.

Understanding and accepting this calling can provide the practicing teacher the most precious of all opportunities, and ones that the academics do not, and cannot have: to use their scholarship, study, and knowledge of deep theoretical work to not only discuss and expound, but to affect others and, therefore, to affect society.

What often prevents teachers from thinking of themselves as scholars, or more specifically social scientists, is the relative "bubble" in which education, as well as educational policy, is often practiced. That is, while education is talked about and acted upon from a variety of perspectives, teachers are often relegated to playing a singular role: teaching.

Of course, those of us who are teachers know that teaching is in no way a singular role, though the influence of external factors, especially those that are divorced from direct knowledge and experience of classroom practice, can often make teaching feel that way. How, then, might teachers begin to act in the role of social scientists?

One way in which practicing teachers may begin to do this is to think of themselves also as anthropologists, perhaps even "educational anthropologists." Educational anthropologist Norma Gonzalez puts it like this:

> Anthropology of education [begins by] asking . . . how and why do human beings educate the way they do? Within this broad purview, the process of education can be defined as humanity's unique methods of teaching and learning—that is, of acquiring, transmitting, producing, and transforming cultural knowledge for interpreting and acting on the world. Anthropologists of education seek to understand how teaching and learning are organized socially and culturally, but teaching and learning encounters are embedded within social processes, and basic theoretical processes cannot be decontextualized from political and applied questions.[6]

In this context the cultural narrative again becomes central to the questions of education, this time deepening to the point of its application to the definition of knowledge in and of itself. That is, not what is teaching and learning, but what is teaching and learning in the context of different cultural narratives, and how can they all be valued as legitimate, important, and worthy of discussion?

Similarly, Apple asks us to consider similar questions, this time with direct relation to power and decision-making latitude in the educational process:

> Whose knowledge is this? How did it become official? What is the relationship between this knowledge and the ways in which it is taught and evaluated, and who has cultural, social, and economic capital in this society? Who benefits from these definitions of legitimate knowledge and from the ways schooling

and this society is organized, and who does not? How do what are usually seen as "reforms" actually work?[7]

From this perspective our practices as teachers are framed not by content or standard-driven perspectives, but rather by political, social, and cultural perspectives, allowing us to view education and schooling not simply as transmission of academic information, but rather active places out of which culture is built. The way in which power, information, knowledge, privilege, and marginalization occur in the schoolhouse is the way in which these processes occur, and will continue to occur, in the culture should they remain unchallenged.

Therefore, the role of the teacher as social scientist becomes directly engaged with the role of the teacher as activist and advocate. As Apple further explores:

> What can we do as critical educators, researchers, and activists to change existing social and educational inequalities and create curricula and teaching that are more socially just?[8]

These are the questions posed not by "mere" classroom teachers, but by informed, educated, trained, and engaged professionals who have been given the responsibility to tend to the future on a moment-to-moment basis with its very participants. This is the charge of the most important job in existence.

In this sense, teachers become the embodiment of what has been called, in multiple variations, the "public intellectual." That is, the purveyor of the best information from scholarly works of inquiry, practical works of application, and experience. But what is the role and responsibility of the public intellectual? Many scholars have tried to make sense of this question in the past.

Antonio Gramsci, an Italian political activist to whom the idea is credited, distinguished between "traditional intellectuals," or those whose role remains largely theoretical and unapplied to critical social situations, and "organic intellectuals," who are created by the need for social change, and who apply their knowledge of theory and research to directly affect the society.[9] Pierre Bourdieu suggests that public intellectuals belong to both "dual and dueling" worlds; one in which theory is prized, such as the academy, and one in which action is prized, such as political activism. As he states:

> On the one hand [intellectuals] must belong to an autonomous intellectual world . . . on the other [the intellectual] must invest the competence and authority . . . acquired in the intellectual field in a political action.[10]

Michael Berubé takes a somewhat different approach, from which he suggests:

> The future of our ability to produce new knowledges for and about ordinary people—and the availability of education to ordinary people—may well depend on how effectively we can . . . make our work intelligible to non-academics.[11]

In this sense, Berubé, similarly to Gramsci, regards the role of the intellectual to form "new knowledges" that, by nature, will challenge and disrupt the old forms of knowledge. But perhaps the most well-known account of the public intellectual comes from Noam Chomsky, noted scholar and social activist, who posits:

> In the Western world, at least, they have the power that comes from political liberty, from access to information and freedom of expression. For a privileged minority, Western democracy provides the leisure, the facilities, and the training to seek the truth lying hidden behind the veil of distortion and misrepresentation, ideology and class interest, through which the events of current history are presented to us. The responsibilities of intellectuals, then, are much deeper than . . . the "responsibility of people," given the unique privileges that intellectuals enjoy.[12]

Here the political intent of intellectuals is not only emphasized but seen as obligatory. An intellectual who does not use his or her intellect to challenge that which is false is, essentially, betraying his or her responsibility as an intellectual.

PRACTICE: TEACHERS AS SOCIAL SCIENTISTS

Ms. K has always regarded herself as a "history and politics" buff, though her subject area is mathematics. She's recently been reading books written by "critical education theorists" who write about deep critiques of capitalism and "neoliberal politics." She's struggling to determine how to incorporate some of these ideas into her class, and whether she has the right to anyway.

1. Have you ever thought about the role of a teacher as a social scientist? Do you agree with this characterization? Why or why not?
2. Think about some of the questions posed in the text above by Gonzalez and Apple. Discuss these a bit.
3. Consider the various conceptualizations of the "public intellectual." Which ones make the most sense to you? Which ones do not? What would you change about them? Critique and discuss each definition in isolation as well as in relation to one another.
4. What are your thoughts about likening the role of the teacher to that of a public intellectual?

TEACHERS AS ACTIVISTS

Extended from the notion of public intellectual is a clear call to action. It is not enough, then, to simply recognize social inequalities from a theoretical perspective and do nothing; neither is it acceptable to become merely an "armchair activist" who calls for action through nonactive means. Rather, teachers who accept their role as scholars must also accept their binary role as activists, hence becoming scholar-activists, or those that use their scholarly knowledge to effect change in the culture directly. Laurence Cox provides a relevant framework from which teachers can begin to see the difference between scholarship and scholarship activism. He explains:

> The work of academics is shaped primarily by the social relations significant in academia, such as employment, academic writing and exposition, credentialing and degree pursuit. Activists, however, function primarily out of relationships in particular social movements. Therefore, scholar-activists use their capital from the academic world to effect change in the social world.[13]

In order to frame what scholarship-activism may look like for teachers, the context of "movement-relevant theory" will be used. Essentially, movement-relevant theory is an attempt to connect the academic participants in social movements with the activist participants in order to produce theories about action that are both scholastically sound and practicable. As Bevington and Dixon suggest:

> Activists are reading academic social histories. But rather than reading the dominant social movement theory, they are generating theory largely outside of academic circles. This is important and valuable. Yet we also want to argue for the value of academic social movement theory that is useful to movements.[14]

This type of framework is ideal for practicing teachers as they have (or can easily have) direct access to legitimate academic resources through libraries, online resources, colleges, and universities, but also have direct access to the "ground" of the movements, which takes place largely in the classroom and communities in which they teach. Essentially, teachers can be the penultimate scholar-activists, capable of making the most amount of change.

To merely consider oneself as part of a movement, however, is not sufficient to be an actual player. As Bevington and Dixon further advise:

> To produce movement-relevant theory, it is not enough to simply identify with a movement or study a movement. Instead, there is a distinct process that involves a dynamic engagement with movements in the formulation, production, refinement, and application of the research . . . the researcher should not have

PRACTICE: TEACHERS AS ACTIVISTS

Mr. L has always considered himself a political person and has been involved in a number of political groups involving the environment, voting rights, and censorship. However, he has always been wary to become directly involved in educational issues for fear of administrative retaliation. Some of his colleagues, however, are beginning to show more of an interest in becoming involved in some upcoming demonstrations.

1. Have you ever considered yourself as an activist in direct relation to being a teacher?
2. Do you think that teachers are obligated to be activists in one way or another? How?
3. Think of an example of something you would consider a "movement" in education. What qualifies it as a movement? How did it develop?
4. If you could give a name and a basic mission for the "education-based" movement you consider yourself a part of, what would it be?

> a detached relation to the movement. Rather, the researcher's connection to the movement provides important incentives to produce more accurate information.[15]

In this sense the distinction between scholars and activists is blurred. That is, scholars are dependent on the activists and the activists are dependent on the scholars. In order for the movements to progress both systematically and positively, there is a need for both theory-based and action-based participation.

Becoming involved in a movement, however, can be risky, and may often be associated with being an ideologue of sorts. That is, when one becomes a *part* of a movement, he or she will become associated with the basic common denominator of that movement, which may or may not accurately reflect the fullness of one's perspective.

Individual voices within a movement, then, are imperative to the growth and development of that movement, and movements that can tolerate, incorporate, and grow from dissenting ideas without fracturing will lead to even stronger movements. This is a cornerstone of movement-relevant theory, whose purpose is not public relations and image building, but true social change, even when that change is difficult, dirty, and dicey. Turning again to Bevington and Dixon:

> Movement-related theory should not, and indeed *cannot* [italics in original], be uncritical adulation of a favored movement . . . such an approach does not

provide it with any useful information and does not aid the movement in identifying and addressing problems which may hinder its effectiveness.[16]

Teachers are individuals, and individuals will have differences, sometimes small and sometimes great. But it is equally true that teachers have a genuinely common goal, which revolves around the edification and success of their students. Indeed, the definitions of edification and success may in themselves differ, perhaps significantly. However, collaboratively working with these differing ideas toward the common goal can also be quite unifying.

MOVEMENT-RELEVANT THEORY IN EDUCATION

What might movements, then, have to do with the reflective teacher? First and foremost, movements are, in a sense, mobilizations of reflection. That is, movements only exist in order to change current states. Whether those changes are to be seen as conservative or progressive may inform the content and context of the change, but they are based on some process of reflection and problem-solving. A problem, or series of problems, has been identified, solutions are formulated and proposed, and a movement is put in place in order to enact those solutions in some sort of practice or policy.

Educational movements, at heart, are made up of reflective teachers, parents, students, and other stakeholders. So how might reflective teachers begin to engage in movement-relevant theory directly? Essentially, Bevington and Dixon suggest three main activities in which activists can engage in order to begin.

First, teachers must locate and name the central and essential issues and questions affecting education. Once located, organized discussion among stakeholders (teachers, parents, students, administrators, and other community members) must be held. These initial meetings should be information-gathering and be conducted with as little judgment and conflict as possible.

Indeed, scholar-activists must know, at the beginning, the current state of the thoughts and opinions within the larger community, whether or not they agree or are happy with the outcome of such exploration. Once these discussions have concluded, scholar-activists must categorize the issues and determine which are global and which are localized, and to what subsets are the localized issues relevant.

Second, relevant research must be conducted that can inform the movement critically. That is, it is not valuable to simply produce research that validates the central themes and tenets of the movement. Rather, research involving identifying central disagreements, themes of opposition, locations

PRACTICE: ENGAGING IN MOVEMENT-RELEVANT THEORY

1. Try to compile a list of three or four essential issues and questions facing education today. This can be in specific reference to your community, school, classrooms, etc. See if you can come to a consensus.
2. Try to anticipate some potential viewpoints that certain "segments" of the community may have (for example, how might administrators, parents, or community members without children in school view this problem?).
3. Try to anticipate some potential disagreements between these parties (for example, what may be some differences between the way an administrator and a community member without children in school view an issue?).
4. Finally, try to come up with some important areas of theory that may inform activities in education activism.

of opposition, and the like must also be engaged and conducted as objectively as possible in order to understand them. Indeed, cavorting with like-minded people alone can give the highly false impression that the values of a movement are more universally accepted than they actually are.

Third, activities that connect the scholarly end of the movement with the action-based end of the movement must be organized and orchestrated. Indeed, these two components of the movement must be regarded as equally important and engage in shared governance, decision-making, and influence over the movement. Clear guidelines, to the extent possible, of how ideas are shared and considered will allow deep and genuine progress of the movement.

NOTES

1. Ralph Waldo Emerson. "To Laugh Often and Much." Retrieved October 13, 2019, from https://www.goodreads.com/quotes/357811-to-know-even-one-life-has-breathed-easier-because-you.
2. Michael W. Apple. (2010). "Putting Critical Back into Educational Research." *Educational Researcher*, *39*(2), 152–162.
3. Michaela Borg. (2004). "The Apprenticeship of Observation." *ELT Journal*, *58*(3).
4. *Ibid.*
5. L. R. Frey & K. M. Carragee. (2007). "Introduction: Communication Activism as Engaged Scholarship." In L. R. Frey & K. M. Carragee (Eds.), *Communication Activism* (pp. 1–64). Cresskill, NJ: Hampton Press.

6. Norma Gonzalez. (2010). "Advocacy Anthropology and Education: Working through the Binaries." *Cultural Anthropology, 51*(2), 249–258.

7. Apple, 2010, p. 152.

8. *Ibid.*

9. Antonio Gramsci. (1971). *Selections from Prison Notebooks*. London: Lawrence & Wishart.

10. Pierre Bourdieu. (1991). "Fourth Lecture: Universal Corporatism: The Role of Intellectuals in a Modern World." *Poetics Today*, *12*(4), 655–669.

11. Michael Berubé. (1994). *Public Access: Literary Theory and American Cultural Politics.* London: Verso.

12. Noam Chomsky. (1967, February). "A Special Supplement: The Responsibility of Intellectuals." *The New York Review of Books.*

13. Laurence Cox. (2015). "Scholarship and Activism: A Social Movements Perspective." *Studies in Social Justice, 9*(1), 34–53.

14. Douglas Bevington & C. Dixon. (2005). "Movement Relevant Theory: Rethinking Social Movement and Scholarship Activism." *Social Movement Studies*, *4*(3), 185–208.

15. *Ibid.*, p. 191.

16. *Ibid.*

Chapter Nine

What Don't I Know Yet?

Engaging Perpetually as a Reflective Teacher

"We are drowning in information, but starved for knowledge."[1]

—John Naisbitt

Because movement-relevant theory centers on a cooperative process between scholars and activists, the goal in education is to find a means of practice that serves to develop theory in a scholarly manner as well as service and social change in an activist-based manner. Finding such a methodology will allow teachers to more readily fulfill their role as scholar-activists within one comprehensive space.

The two modalities targeted in this chapter, which are not mutually exclusive nor the only options, are action research and service learning. Indeed, action research is less an educational methodology than a manner of exploring outcomes in practice-based professions in a more systematic manner than informal observation allows. Pairing this approach with service learning, a method that emphasizes learning about and serving the needs of a particular community by immersing oneself in it, will allow reflective teachers to more readily fulfill their roles as scholar-activists.

ACTION RESEARCH AND THE REFLECTIVE TEACHER

Throughout this book the case for becoming a reflective teacher has been made from a number of different perspectives. Methods by which one could not only be, but act, as a reflective teacher have also been proposed. As a final means of attempting to connect the teacher as a practitioner to his or her dual role as a social scientist, and how this connection can inform teacher identity, the concept of action research will be presented as the most relevant means by which teachers could continuously engage in reflective practice while simultaneously serving the movement of which they see themselves as a part.

Action research has been shown to be an effective and participant-driven means by which teachers can gain greater understanding of their practices while also learning how to serve their students and communities more appropriately and effectively. Research supports this idea by demonstrating that action research contributes to reflective practice by engaging teachers in more systematic inquiry into their own practice, provides grounded means by which teachers could change the elements of their practice that needed to be changed, and provides a collaborative environment in which critical reflection could take place among other engaged practitioners.[2]

As is the case with many other concepts in education, a multitude of definitions attempt to capture what action research is. One definition conceptualizes action research as a way to promote a cycle of improvement that requires the description of a problem, a review of past research investigating that problem, collecting and analyzing new data, using the data analysis to design a new strategy for change, and collecting and analyzing more data to evaluate the new strategy.

Another definition situates action research as a systematic inquiry through which educational stakeholders such as administrators, teachers, and students gather information about how their school operates, how they teach, and how well their students learn.[3]

Whatever definition one eventually adopts, the primary goal of effective action research is to serve a particular, well-structured and well-defined purpose that will serve the needs of the stakeholders directly, not as an exercise in data collection and analysis for its own sake, but to ameliorate legitimate systematic social problems and create safer, more constructive, and more productive spaces for all stakeholders, especially students. Noted reflective teaching scholars Ken Zeichner and Jennifer Gore suggest:

> [Teachers should be concerned with] encouraging action research that contributes toward the elimination of the social conditions that distort self-understandings of teachers and undermine the educative potential and moral base of schooling and teacher education.[4]

A foundation for beginning to view the teacher as researcher can be found from Lawrence Stenhouse, who first proposed the idea in the 1980s. For Stenhouse, the role of the learner, be they a child or adult, is to produce knowledge or ideas that are perpetually open for debate. Therefore, the teacher must facilitate ways in which the learner can research and revise his or her own knowledge while the teacher simultaneously does the same, creating a deeply reflective and research-based learning environment.

This perpetual process of researching is the only means by which both teachers and students can loosen the constraints placed upon them by habits, experiences, and cultural narratives from the past.[5] Given that action research is a key component in facilitating the connection between reflective practices and resulting action, it is important to understand some different approaches to engaging action research.

Ruth Leitch and Christopher Day propose that there are three specific types of action research. Technical action research is focused on conducting inquiry in order to improve the efficiency and effectiveness of teacher skill. For example, "what is the most effective way to teach sight words?" While based on a systematic method of inquiry, this type of research largely situates the teacher as the research participant rather than facilitator, and aims to be prescriptive rather than reflective.

Practical action research aims for a converse goal, in which the inquiry is intended to lead to a deepening of teacher judgment and accumulated personal wisdom. These approaches may be more open and observatory, valuing order and fidelity to methods less than attention to individual expertise and professional behavior that lead to theoretical development. Finally, emancipatory action research is conducted with the direct goal of finding classroom

PRACTICE: BEING AN ACTION RESEARCHER

When Ms. B was an undergraduate in psychology she worked as a lab assistant for one of her professors. She was always fascinated by the research process, and how much her professor learned about human behavior. Since she's become a teacher she has always wanted to find a way to implement research, but since she's in a classroom, not a lab, figures there is no way to really do that.

1. Have you ever engaged in research of any kind in the past, either as a student or a teacher? What did it involve? What was the research about? What were your thoughts about the process?
2. Does your school deal with research in any way? If so, how?
3. As are many concepts in education, action research is defined in multiple ways. Consider the different definitions proposed. Which do you agree with most? What would you add or delete from these definitions to make it better?
4. What might participatory action research look like in your school or classroom? What issues might come up that affect you and your students directly?

practices that can free teachers and students from the compulsive and perfunctory use of traditional instructional practices.[6]

In the vein of emancipatory action research, one methodology that is aimed at disrupting and challenging traditional approaches to education, especially those that recreate and reinforce social inequalities, is known as participatory action research. This type of research seeks to empower both teacher and student as the main researchers, with a particular goal of promoting more democratic and equitable practices in education.[7] Bijoy Barua conceptualizes:

> [Participatory action research is] an active process in which disadvantaged groups are empowered through collective education and partnership . . . committed toward structural social change . . . [and] allows marginalized people to generate their own knowledge from their daily experiences to liberate them from social oppression.[8]

Teachers and students alike can engage in this approach of action research in order to continue to understand the way power dynamics work in culture and society.

SERVICE LEARNING AS SCHOLAR ACTIVISM

Because participatory action research is specifically designed to empower those who have been marginalized by allowing them to generate their own culturally relevant knowledge, this approach is particularly useful to implement in tandem with service learning. While not the only form of "out-of-the-classroom" learning methodologies, service learning is unique in that it possesses a deeply social and cultural component that is steeped in serving marginalized communities directly by working alongside their members, not just on their behalf or at their behest. Catherine Berger Kaye defines:

> [Service learning is] an instructional approach that encourages students to apply their knowledge about pedagogy to real-life situations within a community setting with benefits to both the community and the student. While developing their professional skills, students engaging with service learning gain a deeper understanding of themselves, their community, and society as a whole.[9]

Deborah Biss Keller defines service learning in a more directly culturally based context:

> [It] engages students working with adults in the community in order to learn more about the community . . . and residents' funds of knowledge . . . in which

> [people in the neighborhoods] are seen predominantly through their strengths and their assets . . . in direct contrast to deficit theories, which hold that minority, low-income children . . . are linguistically or cognitively lacking or that they are culturally deficient . . . [which] fails to acknowledge systemic and structural inequities at work including inequities in education and basic human rights.[10]

Because service learning directly challenges and disrupts the stronghold of dominant cultural narratives, especially in its more negative aspects of cultural deficiency conceptualizations, teachers have no choice but to reflect on how their own preconceptions are at work, and how these preconceptions encompass these narratives.

Service learning does more, however, than just test teachers' preconceptions from their own cultural narratives. It further challenges them to reevaluate the teaching philosophies and methodologies they were exposed to in their teacher education programs, and explore whether these pedagogies simply reproduced and reinforced these narratives, or whether they were indeed emancipatory and socially just. As Ellen Cushman suggests:

> Service learning asks students . . . to test the merit of what they learn in the university classroom against their experience . . . at local sites. Students enter the community in a sincere effort to both engage in and observe language use that helps address the topics that are important to community members . . . students and community members can develop reciprocal and dialogic relations with each other [and] their relationship is a mutually beneficial give-and-take one.[11]

In this light, service learning is, by design, reflective as one is consistently challenged to hold his or her previously held beliefs in dialectic with the means by which a community actually functions. Therefore, the reproduction of knowledge and practice is not left to its own devices; rather, it is perpetually reflected upon, reformed, and revised in accordance with actual community needs rather than pedantic conservation.

Essentially, service learning seeks to reengage youth, and by extension their teachers, in civic engagement, allowing for increased trust and connection to be built with one's surrounding communities, specifically those with which prior engagement was limited, or even discouraged. Indeed, in a stratified society that has a deep basis in race, ethnicity, and class, such separation of communities is likely to fall along these very lines.

This separation of communities allows the misconceptions of dominant cultural narratives to remain unchallenged and central in one's thinking and perception of the communities, perpetuating and reproducing myths and causing a threat to democracy. Service learning addresses this separation directly by instilling such civic and citizenship values as self-concept, or an understanding of who one is, political engagement, or faith in participating in the political system to enact change, and tolerance, or being comfortable with the expression of views, beliefs, and actions that may not be aligned with one's own thoughts, but are permissible so long as they are not harmful or hurtful.

William Morgan and Matthew Streb put it this way:

> If students are involved in service learning projects in which they have a high degree of voice and ownership, their self-concept and political engagement will improve, and they will become more tolerant toward out-groups. In short, having a voice in service learning builds citizenship.[12]

Jennifer Ashton and Hannah Arlington demonstrate both the personal and professional benefit of service learning in the area of working with people with disabilities. Through a service learning project connected with the education department at their college, students were required to have direct engagement with people with disabilities in their community rather than in the classroom. In this context, the power dynamic was equalized, as both parties were now simply engaging as individuals rather than in a teacher-student or clinician-client capacity.

When surveyed before the initiation of the project, participants in the class noted themes such as fear, expertise, conceptions of disability, presumptions of incompetence, and thoughts about inclusion, many of which were framed in a negative and critical perspective. After completing the project, however, many of the participants reevaluated and reformed their initial thoughts to become far more positive, accepting, and humbling. As the authors note:

> Teacher candidates [had] considered the formal legal and structural aspects of special education and found that this provides only one perspective on teaching students with disabilities. They have acknowledged that their preconceived notions of disability have been shaped by the traditional special education system. Through their involvement with the service learning project, they have gained a new understanding of the importance of human interaction and learning about the person . . . and have begun to see their own misconceptions more clearly.[13]

Clearly, exposure to individuals in environments that are more naturalistic, if not "home-based" for the marginalized community, can effectively challenge and change misconceptions shaped by dominant cultural narratives, allowing the teacher to become more open to the idea of "not knowing," a key component of meaningful reflection. While this process can be difficult to convince one to engage in, it is the very heart of reflective teaching.

When one consistently exposes one's preconceptions to critique there is no other outcome possible than a deepening of one's teaching capability, and making a practice of this will ensure that the teacher remains a learner

PRACTICE: SERVICE LEARNING

Though Mrs. B is white, she lives in a part of the city that is predominantly black and Hispanic because it is closer to the train she takes to see her parents. She has always been treated well and her neighbors are friendly, but she always felt there was more that she could be doing to engage. She wondered, though, whether her skin color would be an obstacle, and her efforts seen only as charitable, not genuine community engagement.

1. What elements of service learning have you already implemented in your classroom? These may not be "full-fledged" projects, but in what ways have you attempted to connect classroom learning to the community?
2. What might service learning look like in your community? What types of environments would be most beneficial for your students to engage in, and for you as a teacher to experience?
3. How would you distinguish your students' service work from "charity" work? That is, how would you ensure that there is an equal power dynamic between your students and the community members, with community members serving as "real-life" educators, not just recipients of service?

for the duration of his or her career. This example shows that students can even exceed the virtue of tolerance, as proposed by Morgan and Streb, and attain something closer to value, allowing them to not only passively accept a different culture's presence, but value and incorporate its contributions to society actively.

NOTES

1. John Naisbitt. (1982). *Megatrends: Ten New Directions Transforming Our Lives*. New York: Warner Books.
2. Rita Hagevik, M. Aydeniz, & C. Glennon Rowell. (2012). "Using Action Research in Middle Level Teacher Education to Evaluate and Deepen Reflective Practice." *Teaching and Teacher Education*, *28*(5), 675–684.
3. *Ibid.*
4. Kenneth Zeichner & J. Gore. (1995). "Using Action Research as a Vehicle for Student Reflection." In S. Noffke & R. B. Stevenson (Eds.). *Educational Action Research*. New York: Teachers College Press.
5. Martyn Hemmersley. (1993). "On the Teacher as Researcher." *Education Action Research*, *1*(3), 425–445.
6. Ruth Leitch & C. Day. (2000). "Action Research and Reflective Practice: Towards a Holistic View." *Educational Action Research, 8*(1), 179–193.

7. Marina-Stefania Giannakaki, I. D. McMillan, & J. Karamichas. (2018). "Problematizing the Use of Education to Address Social Inequity: Could Participatory Action Research Be a Step Forwards?" *British Educational Research Journal*, *44*(2), 191–211.

8. Bijoy P. Barua. (2009). "Participatory Action Research, NGOs, and Grassroots Development: Challenges in Rural Bangladesh." In D. Kapoor & S. Jordan (Eds.), *Education, Participatory Action Research, and Social Change: International Perspectives* (pp. 239–250). New York: Palgrave Macmillan.

9. Catherine Berger Kaye (2010) as cited by Jennifer Randhare Ashton & H. Arlington. (2019). "My Fears Were Irrational: Transforming Conceptions of Disability in Teacher Education Through Service Learning." *International Journal of Whole Schooling*, *15*(1), 50–81.

10. Deborah Biss Keller. (2019). "Requisite Community Engagement for Teacher Education: A Different Take on Service Learning." *Athens Journal of Education*, *6*(2), 93–110.

11. Ellen Cushman. (1999). "The Public Intellectual, Service Learning, and Activist Research." *College English*, *61*(3), 328–337.

12. William Morgan & M. Streb. (2001). "Building Citizenship: How Student Voice in Service Learning Develops Civic Values." *Social Science Quarterly*, *82*(1), 154–169.

13. Jennifer Randhare Ashton & H. Arlington. (2019). "My Fears Were Irrational: Transforming Conceptions of Disability in Teacher Education through Service Learning." *International Journal of Whole Schooling, 15*(1), 68.

Bibliography

Alsup, Janet. "Am I a Teacher? Exploring the Development of Professional Identity." *Language Arts Journal of Michigan*, 20, no. 1 (2004): 35–39.

Apple, Michael W. "Putting Critical Back into Educational Research." *Educational Researcher*, 39, no. 2 (2010): 152–162.

Ashton, Jennifer Randhare, & H. Arlington. "My Fears Were Irrational: Transforming Conceptions of Disability in Teacher Education through Service Learning." *International Journal of Whole Schooling*, 15, no. 1 (2019): 50–81.

Barua, Bijoy P. (2009). "Participatory Action Research, NGOs, and Grassroots Development: Challenges in Rural Bangladesh." In D. Kapoor & S. Jordan (Eds.), *Education, Participatory Action Research, and Social Change: International Perspectives* (pp. 239–250). New York: Palgrave Macmillan.

Bauer, Jack, & D. McAdams. "Personal Growth in Adults' Stories of Life Transitions." *Journal of Personality*, 72, no. 3 (2004): 573–602.

Beauchamp, Catherine, & L. Thomas. "Understanding Teacher Identity: An Overview of Issues in the Literature and Implications for Teacher Education." *Cambridge Journal of Education*, 39, no. 2 (2009): 175–189.

Begley, Paul T. (2003). "In Pursuit of Authentic School Leadership Practices." In Paul T. Begley & O. Johansson (Eds.), *The Ethical Dimensions of School Leadership* (pp. 1–12). Netherlands: Kluwer.

Berubé, Michael. *Public Access: Literary Theory and American Cultural Politics*. London: Verso, 1994.

Bevington, Douglas, & C. Dixon. "Movement Relevant Theory: Rethinking Social Movement and Scholarship Activism." *Social Movement Studies*, 4, no. 3 (2005): 185–208.

Bilbao, P. P., P. I. Lucido, T. C. Iringan, & R. B. Javier. *Curriculum Development*. Philippines: Lorimar Publishing Inc., 2008.

Biss Keller, Deborah. "Requisite Community Engagement for Teacher Education: A Different Take on Service Learning." *Athens Journal of Education*, 6, no. 2 (2019): 93–110.

Black, William. (2014, December). "How Watermelons Became a Racist Trope." *The Atlantic*.

Bobek, Becky L. "Teacher Resiliency: A Key to Career Longevity." *The Clearing House*, 75, no. 4 (2002): 202–205.

Borg, Michaela. "The Apprenticeship of Observation." *ELT Journal*, 58, no. 3 (2004): 274–276.

Bourdieu, Pierre. "Fourth Lecture: Universal Corporatism: The Role of Intellectuals in a Modern World." *Poetics Today*, 12, no. 4 (1991): 655–669.

Brown, Dave F. "Management Strategies: Reflection of Culturally Responsive Teaching." *Urban Education*, 39, no. 3 (2004): 266–289.

Brown, Monica R. "Educating All Students: Creating Culturally Responsive Teachers, Classrooms, and Schools." *Intervention in School & Clinic*, 43, no. 1 (2007): 57–62.

Budak, Ceren, S. Goel, & J. Rao. "Fair and Balanced: Quantifying Media Bias through Crowdsourced Content Analysis." *Public Opinion Quarterly*, 80, no. 1 (2016): 250–271.

Butt, Richard, & J. Retalik. "Professional Well-Being and Learning: A Study of Administrator-Teacher Workplace Relationships." *Journal of Educational Enquiry*, 3, no. 1 (2002): 17–34.

Castro, Antonio, J. Kelly, & M. Shih. "Resilience Strategies for New Teachers in High-Needs Areas." *Teaching and Teacher Education*, 22 (2010): 622–629.

Chomsky, Noam. (1967, February). "A Special Supplement: The Responsibility of Intellectuals." *The New York Review of Books*.

Coelho, Paulo. *The Alchemist*. New York: HarperOne, 1993.

Cole, Michael, J. Gay, J. Glick, & D. W. Sharp. *The Cultural Context of Learning and Thinking*. New York: Basic Books, 1971.

Cox, Laurence. "Scholarship and Activism: A Social Movements Perspective." *Studies in Social Justice*, 9, no. 1 (2015): 34–53.

Cushman, Ellen. "The Public Intellectual, Service Learning, and Activist Research." *College English*, 61, no. 3 (1999): 328–337.

Danesh, H. B. "Towards an Integrative Theory of Peace Education." *Journal of Peace Education*, 3, no. 1 (2006): 55–78.

Das, Lama Surya. *Awakening the Buddhist Heart: Integrating Love, Meaning, and Connection into Every Part of Your Life*. New York: Potter/Ten Speed/Harmony/Rosedale, 2007.

Delpit, Lisa. "Lessons from Teachers." *Journal of Teacher Education*, 57, no. 3 (2006): 220–231.

Emerson, Ralph Waldo. "To Laugh Often and Much." From https://www.goodreads.com/quotes/357811-to-know-even-one-life-has-breathed-easier-because-you.

Farah, Iffat. (1998). "The Ethnography of Communication." In N. H. Horenberger & P. Corson (Eds.), *Encyclopedia of Language and Education: Volume 8: Research Methods in Language and Communication* (pp. 125–133). Dordrecht, Netherlands: Kluwer.

Fivush, Robyn, T. Habermas, T. E. A. Waters et al. "The Making of Autobiographical Memory: Intersections of Culture, Narrative, and Identity." *International Journal of Psychology*, 46, no. 5 (2011): 321–345.

Flintoff, Anne, A. Chappell, C. Gower et al. "Black and Minority Ethnic Trainees' Experiences of Physical Education Initial Teacher Training." *Report to the Training and Development Agency, Carnegie Institute, Leeds Metropolitan University*. From https://bura.brunel.ac.uk/bitstream/2438/4693/1/Fulltext.pdf.

Foucault, Michel. *The Use of Pleasure: A History of Sexuality, Vol II*. London, UK: Harmondsworth, Penguin, 1992.

Franklin, John H., G. Horne, H. Cruse, A. Ballard, & R. Mitchell Jr. "Black History Month: Serious Truth Telling or a Triumph in Tokenism." *Journal of Blacks in Higher Education*, 18 (1997): 87–92.

Frey, L. R., & K. M. Carragee. (2007). "Introduction: Communication Activism as Engaged Scholarship." In L. R. Frey & K. M. Carragee (Eds.), *Communication Activism* (pp. 1–64). Cresskill, NJ: Hampton Press.

Gay, Geneva. "Preparing for Culturally Responsive Teaching." *Journal of Teacher Education*, 53, no. 2 (2002): 106–116.

Gay, Geneva. *Culturally Responsive Teaching: Theory, Research, and Practice*. New York: Teachers College Press, 2000.

Giannakaki, Marina-Stefania, I. D. McMillan, & J. Karamichas. "Problematizing the Use of Education to Address Social Inequity: Could Participatory Action Research Be a Step Forwards?" *British Educational Research Journal*, 44, no. 2 (2018): 191–211.

Gonzalez, Norma. "Advocacy Anthropology and Education: Working through the Binaries." *Cultural Anthropology*, 51, no. 2 (2010): 249–258.

Good, Merle, & Phyllis Good. *20 Most Asked Questions about the Amish and Mennonites*. New York: Simon & Schuster, 2001.

Gramsci, Antonio. *Selections from Prison Notebooks*. London: Lawrence & Wishart, 1971.

Gregory, Anne, R. Skiba, & P. A. Noguera. "The Achievement Gap and the Discipline Gap: Two Sides of the Same Coin?" *Educational Researcher*, 39, no. 1 (2011): 59–68.

Hagevik, Rita, M. Aydeniz, & C. Glennon Rowell. "Using Action Research in Middle Level Teacher Education to Evaluate and Deepen Reflective Practice." *Teaching and Teacher Education*, 28, no. 5 (2012): 675–684.

Hamman, Doug, K. Gosselin, J. Romano et al. "Using Possible Selves Theory to Understand the Identity Development of New Teachers." *Teaching and Teacher Education*, 26 (2010): 1349–1361.

Hargreaves, Andy. "The Emotional Geographies of Teaching." *Teachers College Record*, 103, no. 6 (2001): 1056–1080.

Harris, Ian. "Challenges for Peace Educators at the Beginning of the 21st Century." *Social Alternatives*, 21, no. 1 (2002): 28–31.

Hemmersley, Martyn. "On the Teacher as Researcher." *Education Action Research*, 1, no. 3 (1993): 425–445.

Hochschild, Arlie. *The Managed Heart*. Berkeley: University of California Press, 1983.

Hughes, Amy L., J. J. Matt, & F. L. O'Reilly. "Principal Support Is Imperative to the Retention of Teachers in Hard-to-Staff Schools." *Journal of Education and Training Studies*, 3, no. 1 (2015): 129–134.

Hymes, Dell. (1972). "Models of Interactions of Language and Social Life." In J. Gumperz & D. Hymes (Eds.), *Directions in Sociolinguistics: The Ethnography of Communication* (pp. 35–71). Oxford: Blackwell.

Imada, Toshie. "Cultural Narratives of Individualism and Collectivism: A Content Analysis of Textbook Stories in the United States and Japan." *Journal of Cross-Cultural Psychology*, 43, no. 4 (2012): 576–591.

Jenkins, Tony. (2004). "Comprehensive Programme and Course Planning Frameworks for the University of Peace Master's Degree Programme in Peace Education." Teachers College, Columbia University.

Johnson, David W., & R. T. Johnson. (2010). "Peace Education in the Classroom: Creating Effective Peace Education Programs." In G. Salomon & E. Cairns (Eds.), *Handbook on Peace Education* (pp. 223–240). New York: Psychology Press.

Johnson, David W., & R. T. Johnson. "Essential Components of Peace Education." *Theory into Practice*, 44, no. 4 (2005): 280–292.

Kane, Anne. "Reconstructing Culture in Historical Explanation: Narrative as Cultural Structure and Practice." *History and Theory*, 39 (2000): 311–330.

Kennedy, Sheryl Y., & J. B. Smith. "The Relationship between School Collective Reflective Practice and Teacher Physiological Efficacy Sources." *Teaching and Teacher Education*, 29 (2013): 132–143.

Kester, Kevin. "Peace Education: Experience and Storytelling as Living Education." *Peace & Conflict Review*, 2, no. 2 (2008): 1–14.

Kim, Kyung Hee, & D. Zabelina. "Cultural Bias in Assessment: Can Creativity Assessment Help?" *International Journal of Critical Pedagogy*, 6, no. 2 (2015): 129–148.

King, LaGarrett J., & K. Brown. "Once a Year to Be Black: Fighting Against Typical Black History Month Pedagogies." *Negro Educational Review*, 65 (2014): 23–43.

Kochan, Frances, P. Bredeson, & C. Riehl. "Rethinking Development of School Leaders." *Yearbook for the National Society of the Study of Education*, 101, no. 1 (2005): 289–306.

Kosnik, Lea-Rachel D. "Refusing to Budge: A Confirmatory Bias in Decision Making." *Mind & Society*, 7, no. 2 (2008): 193–214.

Kundera, Milan. *The Unbearable Lightness of Being.* New York: Harper Row, 2004.

Leitch, Ruth, & C. Day. "Action Research and Reflective Practice: Towards a Holistic View." *Educational Action Research*, 8, no. 1 (2000): 179–193.

Lindner, Andrew M., & D. N. Hawkins. "Globalization, Culture Wars, and Attitudes Toward Soccer in America: An Empirical Assessment of How Soccer Explains the World." *The Sociological Quarterly*, 53, no. 1 (2012): 68–91.

Lopez, Gerardo R. "The (Racially Neutral) Politics of Education: A Critical Race Theory Perspective." *Educational Administration Quarterly*, 39, no. 1 (2003): 68–94.

Loughran, J. John. "Effective Reflective Practice: In Search of Meaning in Learning about Teaching." *Journal of Teacher Education*, 53, no. 1 (2002): 33–43.

Luchtenberg, Sigrid. (2006). "Ethnic Diversity and Citizenship in Germany." In J. A. Banks (Ed.), *Diversity and Citizenship Education: Global Perspectives* (pp. 245–271). New York: Jossey-Bass.

Lyons, Christopher J., & E. M. Pettit. "Compounded Disadvantage: Race, Incarceration, and Wage Growth." *Social Problems*, 58, no. 2 (2011): 257–280.

Mambrol, Nasruallah. (2017). "Hegemony." *Literary Theory and Criticism*. From https://literariness.org/2017/10/10/hegemony.

Markus, Hazel, & P. Nurius. "Possible Selves." *American Psychologist*, 41, no. 9 (1986): 954–969.

McLuhan, Marshall. *Understanding Media: The Extensions of Man*. New York: Mentor, 1964.

Monroe, Carla. "African American Boys and the Discipline Gap: Balancing Educators' Uneven Hand." *Educational Horizons*, 84, no. 2 (2006): 102–111.

Morgan, William, & M. Streb. "Building Citizenship: How Student Voice in Service Learning Develops Civic Values." *Social Science Quarterly*, 82, no. 1 (2001): 154–169.

Naisbitt, John. *Megatrends: Ten New Directions Transforming Our Lives*. New York: Warner Books, 1982.

Nelson, Katherine, & R. Fivush. "The Emergence of Autobiographical Memory: A Social Cultural Developmental Theory." *Psychological Review*, 111, no. 2 (2004): 486–511.

Niesche, Richard, & Malcolm Haase. "Emotions and Ethics: A Foucauldian Framework for Becoming and Ethical Educator." *Educational Philosophy and Theory*, 44, no. 3 (2012): 276–288.

Otto, S. J., & M. Arnold. "A Study of Experienced Special Education Teachers' Perceptions of Administrative Support." *College Student Journal*, 39, no. 2 (2005): 253–259.

Pajares, M. Frank. "Teachers' Beliefs and Educational Research: Cleaning Up a Messy Construct." *Review of Educational Research*, 62, no. 3 (1992): 307–332.

Paul-Emile, Kimani. "Beyond Title VII: Rethinking Race, Ex-Offender Status, and Employment Discrimination in the Information Age." *Virginia Law Review*, 100, no. 5 (2014): 893–952.

Peterson, Kent D., & T. E. Deal. *The Shaping of School Culture Fieldbook*. San Francisco: Jossey-Bass, 2002.

Phelan, Sean. (2011). "The Media as Neoliberalized Sediment: Articulating Laclau's Discourse Theory with Bourdieu's Field Theory." In Lincoln Dahlberg and S. Phelan (Eds.), *Discourse Theory and Cultural Media Politics* (pp. 128–153). New York: Springer.

Postman, Neal, & C. Weingartner. *Teaching as a Subversive Activity: A No-Holds-Barred Assault on Outdated Teaching Methods with Dramatic and Practical Proposals on How Education Can Be Made Relevant to Today's World*. New York: Bantam Dell, 1971.

Rappaport, Julian. "Community Narratives: Tales of Terror and Joy." *American Journal of Community Psychology*, 28, no. 1 (2000): 1–24.

Rashbaum, William K., & A. Winston. (2018). "Ilana Glazer Event Canceled After Anti-Semitic Graffiti Is Found." *New York Times*. From https://www.nytimes.com/2018/11/02/nyregion/broad-city-jewish-synagogue-anti-semitism.html.

Ready, Douglas D. "Socioeconomic Disadvantage, School Attendance, and Early Cognitive Development: The Differential Effects of School Exposure." *Sociology of Education*, 83, no. 4 (2010): 271–286.

Richards, Heraldo V., A. Brown, & T. Forde. "Addressing Diversity in Schools: Culturally Responsive Pedagogy." *Teaching Exceptional Children*, 39, no. 3 (2007): 64–68.

Richardson, Virginia. (1996). "The Role of Attitude and Belief in Learning to Teach." In J. Sikula, T. J. Buttery, & E. Guyton (Eds.), *Handbook of Research on Teacher Education*. New York: Simon & Schuster Macmillan.

Rosen, Yigal, & G. Salomon. "Durability of Peace Education in the Shadow of Conflict." *Social Psychology of Education*, 14 (2011): 135–147.

Sachs, Judyth. (2013). "Teacher Education and Development of Professional Identity: Learning to be a Teacher." In P. Denicolo & M. Kompf (Eds.), *Connecting Policy and Practice: Challenges for Teaching and Learning in Schools and Universities* (pp. 5–21). Oxford: Routledge.

Schon, Donald. *The Reflective Practitioner: How Professionals Think in Action*. New York: Basic Books, 1983.

School Superintendents Association. (2018). *2017–2018 AASA Superintendent Salary and Benefits Study*. From https://aasa.org/uploadedFiles/Policy_and_Advocacy/Final%20Report%202017-18%20Non-Member.pdf.

Segall, Jordan. "Mass Incarceration, Ex-Felon Discrimination, and Black Labor Market Disadvantage." *University of Pennsylvania Journal of Law and Social Change*, 14 (2011): 159–182.

Sheets, Tara, & J. D. Gallop. (2017). "Bacon Used in Hate Crime: Titusville Man Gets 15 Years in Mosque Vandalism." *Florida Today*. From https://www.floridatoday.com/story/news/crime/2017/12/05/titusville-man-sentenced-15-years-prison-after-mosque-vandalism/924987001/.

Shields, C. M. "Learning About Assessment from Native American Schools: Advocacy and Empowerment." *Theory into Practice*, 36 (1997): 102–109.

Shyman, Eric. "A Comparison of Concepts of Democracy and Experience in a Sample of Major Works by Dewey and Freire." *Educational Philosophy and Theory*, 43, no. 10 (2011): 1035–1046.

Singer, Jefferson A. "Narrative Identity and Meaning Making Across the Adult Lifespan: An Introduction." *Journal of Personality*, 72, no. 3 (2004): 437–459.

Stoneham, Carlos R. (2015). "The Role of Soccer in Latin American Culture. Soccer Politics: A Discussion Forum about the Power of the Global Game." From https://sites.duke.edu/wcwp/2015/02/06/the-role-of-soccer-in-latin-american-culture/.

Thomas, Duane E., & H. Stevenson. "Gender Risks and Education: The Particular Classroom Challenges of Low-Income African-American Boys." *Review of Research in Education*, 33, no. 1 (2009): 160–180.

Thurman, Robert A. F. "Guidelines for Buddhist Social Activism Based on Nagarjuna's 'Jewel Garland of Royal Counsels.'" *The Tibet Journal*, 11, no. 4 (1986): 8–34.

US Department of Education. (2019). National Center for Education Statistics. (NCES-2018-070).

US Department of Education, National Center for Education Statistics. (2018). *The Condition of Education*. (NCES 2018-144).

US Department of Education (2016). *Trends in Public and Private School Principal Demographics and Qualifications: 1987–1988 and 2011–12.* From https://nces.ed.gov/pubs2016/2016189.pdf.

Vavrus, Michael. (2008). "Culturally Responsive Teaching." In M. Good (Ed.), *21st Century Teaching: A Reference Handbook* (pp. 49–57). Thousand Oaks, CA: Sage.

Wills, John H. "Who Needs Multicultural Education? White Students, US History, and the Construction of a Usable Past." *Anthropology & Education Quarterly*, 27, no. 3 (1996): 365–389.

Wills, John H. "Popular Culture, Curriculum, and Historical Representation: The Situation of Native Americans in History and the Perpetuation of Stereotypes." *Journal of Narrative and Life History*, 4, no. 4 (1994): 277–294.

Yost, Deborah S. "Reflection and Self-Efficacy: Enhancing the Retention of Qualified Teachers from a Teacher Education Perspective." *Teacher Education Quarterly*, 33, no. 4 (2006): 59–76.

Zeichner, K., & J. Gore. (1995). Using Action Research as a Vehicle for Student Reflection. In S. Noffke & R. B. Stevenson (Eds.), *Educational Action Research*. New York: Teachers College Press.

Zeichner, Kenneth M., & D. P. Liston. *Reflective Teaching: An Introduction*. New York: Routledge, 2013.

Zembylas. Michalinos. "Emotions and Teacher Identity: A Poststructural Perspective." *Teachers and Teaching: Theory and Practice*, 9, no. 3 (2003): 214–238.

About the Author

Eric Shyman, EdD, is associate professor of child study at St. Joseph's College in New York, from which he won the Early Career Award in 2014. He received his doctorate degree from Teachers College, Columbia University, in 2009. Publishing widely in national and international peer-reviewed journals, Eric Shyman writes on multiple areas including disability rights, inclusive education, race and ethnicity, schooling inequality, and teaching methodologies. This is his fifth book. His other books include *Beyond Equality in the American Classroom: The Case for Inclusive Education*; *Besieged by Behavior Analysis: A Treatise for Comprehensive Educational Approaches*; *Vicious Circles in Education Reform: Assimilation, Americanization, and Fulfilling the Middle Class Ethic*; and *Reclaiming Our Children, Reclaiming our Schools: Reversing Privatization and Recovering Democracy in America's Public Schools*.